HEINEMANN MATHEMATICS 8

Extension textbook

These are the different types of pages and symbols used in this book:

These pages develop mathematical skills, concepts and facts in a wide variety of realistic contexts.

Detours provide self-contained activities which often require an exploratory, investigative approach drawing on problem-solving skills.

Challenges are more-demanding activities designed to stimulate further thought and discussion.

Investigations enhance the work of the page by providing additional opportunities to develop and use problem-solving skills.

Contents

Try these three puzzles from a school
magazine's *Puzzle Corner*.

Puzzle Corner Issue 5 **Magical Muddle**

In a magic square, each row, column and diagonal adds up to
the same total. Copy each of these magic squares. Complete the
squares using **decimal fractions**.

9·6		
3·6	6	
4·8		

2·46	11·07	4·92
7·38		

4·35		
11·6	1·45	8·7

$2\frac{2}{5}$		
1·8	3	
$4\frac{4}{5}$		

		4·2
$3\frac{3}{10}$	$3\frac{1}{2}$	
2·8		

$1\frac{4}{5}$		
	4·5	
	$\frac{9}{10}$	7·2

Puzzle Corner Issue 8 **Triangular Trouble**

In this puzzle each side of a triangle adds
up to the same total. Find the missing
numbers.

Make a triangle puzzle using only these
numbers.

0·92   1·3   2·49   2·87   3·18   3·56

Puzzle Corner Issue 11 **Pathways**

Follow arrows to reach a target number
of **17·4**.

The order is:

$$11·2 + 2·8 + 3·4 = \mathbf{17·4}$$

1 Write the order for a target number of
   (a) 11·1 **(b)** 4·3

2 Write the order for
   (a) the largest
   (b) the smallest possible target number.

3 Design your own pathways puzzle and
   make up questions for a partner to
   answer.

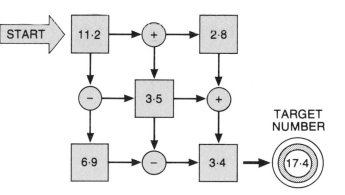

Apollo

These drawings show two of the Saturn rockets used in the Apollo space programme.

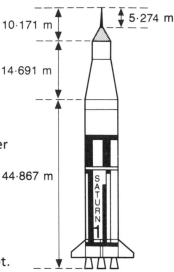

1 Calculate the total length, in metres, of each rocket.

2 The dotted part is the command module which returns to Earth. For each rocket, calculate the length of this module.

3 A 40-storey block of flats is 108 metres high. How much taller is the Saturn 5 rocket?

4 Saturn 1 has a diameter of 6·706 metres.
Saturn 5 has a diameter half as much again.
Calculate the diameter of Saturn 5.

5 The table shows the launch weight in tonnes, for each rocket. How much heavier at launch is Saturn 5?

	Saturn 1	Saturn 5
Launch weight (t)	509·091	2727·270

6 One of the astronauts weighed 73·470 kg before the flight. On returning to Earth he weighed 70·495 kg. Calculate his weight loss.

7 In its first year the space programme cost £7·364 million. The next year it cost £3·896 million **more**. What was the cost in the second year?

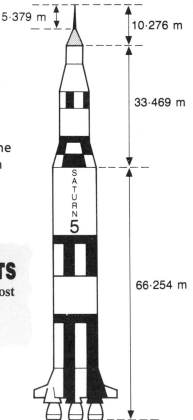

COST OF APOLLO SPACE PROGRAMME ROCKETS

It was announced yesterday that the Apollo space programme has cost a total of £54·1 million since it started four years ago. It was also disclosed that the estimated cost for next year is £37·52 million.

8 Find the average cost per year of the programme for
   (a) the first four years
   (b) the first five years, if the estimated cost reported in the newspaper was correct.

9 The average cost per year for the first five years was actually £20·265 million. Find
   (a) the total cost of the programme over the five years
   (b) the cost in the fifth year
   (c) the difference between the estimated cost and the actual cost for the fifth year.

The length of the Moon Buggy axle must be 0·625±0·002 metres.
This means that
- the longest acceptable length is 0·625+0·002 = 0·627 metres
- the shortest acceptable length is 0·625−0·002 = 0·623 metres.

1 This is an engineering drawing of a
bolt for the Moon Buggy.
  (a) Calculate the longest and shortest
  acceptable lengths.
  (b) Which of these lengths in cm, are **not** acceptable:
  5·240, 5·242, 5·247, 5·250?

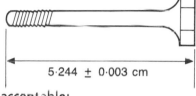

5·244 ± 0·003 cm

2 The data sheet gives information about the lengths of these
Moon Buggy parts. Copy and complete the data sheet.

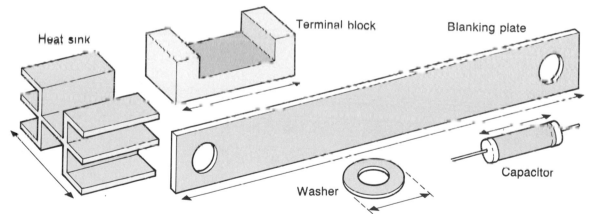

Heat sink

Terminal block

Blanking plate

Washer

Capacitor

Moon Buggy data sheet

Moon Buggy part	Specification in cm	Shortest acceptable length in cm	Longest acceptable length in cm	Difference in cm
Bolt	5·244±0·003	5·241	5·247	0·006
Washer	2·5±0·004	2·496		
Terminal block	15±0·025			
Heat sink		6·155		0·070
Capacitor			3·215	0·030
Blanking plate		29·455	29·545	

Ask your teacher what to do next.

Disco lights

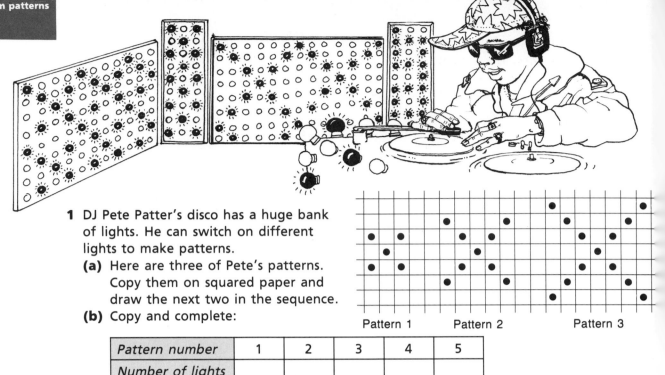

1 DJ Pete Patter's disco has a huge bank of lights. He can switch on different lights to make patterns.

(a) Here are three of Pete's patterns. Copy them on squared paper and draw the next two in the sequence.

(b) Copy and complete:

Pattern 1   Pattern 2   Pattern 3

Pattern number	1	2	3	4	5
Number of lights					

Formula: The number of lights is ▨ times the pattern number, add 1.

2 Find a formula for the number of lights in each of these disco patterns:

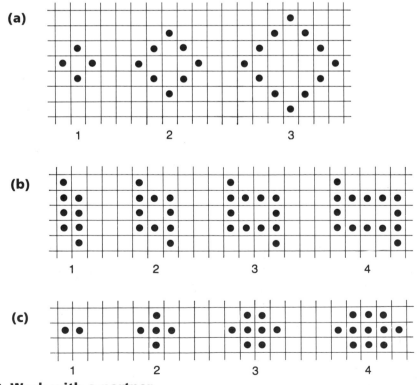

3 Work with a partner.

Make up your own disco light patterns.

Ask your partner to extend your patterns.

Write the formula for the number of lights in each pattern.

Kirsten and Julia pull this raft across the river with a rope. The rope is attached to the raft and passes round poles on either bank. **The raft can only hold one person at a time.**

The raft is at the bank beside Kirsten and Julia. They cross the river like this.

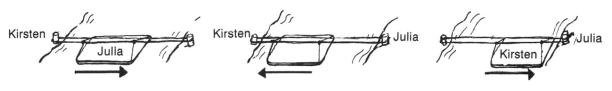

The **raft** crosses 3 times.

Always start with the raft and people on the same bank.

1 How many times does the **raft** cross the river to get
  (a) Kirsten, Julia and Assad across
  (b) Kirsten, Julia, Assad and Dave across
  (c) Kirsten, Julia, Assad, Dave and Assifa across?

2 Copy and complete the table.

Number of people (p)	1	2	3	4	5
Number of raft crossings (c)		3			

The increase in the number of raft crossings each time is **2**.
The number of raft crossings (c) is **2** times the number of people (p) subtract **1**.

This formula in letters is $c = 2p - 1$

3 Here is part of a bridge made from 4 supports and 12 planks.

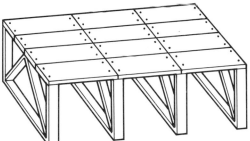

(a) Copy and complete:

Number of supports (s)	2	3	4	5	6	7
Number of planks (p)			12			

(b) Write a formula for the number of planks
  ● in words ● in letters.

Tony the landscape gardener

Tony designs gardens based on square
flower beds and grey and white slabs.
He uses a formula to work out the
number of slabs he will need for each
pattern.

1 Here is one of Tony's designs.

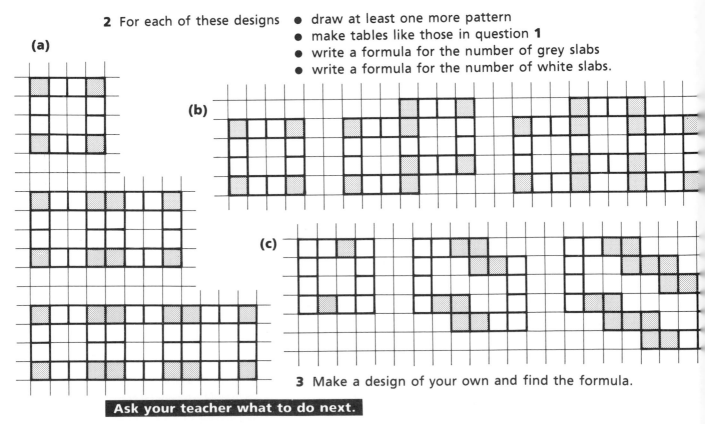

(a) Draw the fourth pattern.
(b) Copy and complete the tables.

Number of flower beds (f)	1	2	3	4
Number of grey slabs (g)	4	6		

Number of flower beds (f)	1	2	3	4
Number of white slabs (w)	8	14		

(c) Write a formula for
  ● the number of grey slabs   ● the number of white slabs.

(d) Use the formulae to find
  ● the number of grey slabs Tony
    needs for the pattern with seven
    flower beds
  ● the number of white slabs Tony
    needs for the pattern with
    twelve flower beds.

2 For each of these designs   ● draw at least one more pattern
                                  ● make tables like those in question **1**
                                  ● write a formula for the number of grey slabs
                                  ● write a formula for the number of white slabs.

(a)

(b)

(c)

3 Make a design of your own and find the formula.

Ask your teacher what to do next.

ACROSS 2 On horseback (5) **DOWN** 1 Infant (4)
6 Film premiere (4) 2 Telephoned (4)

The first crossword puzzle, designed by Arthur Wynne, was published in America on 21 December 1913. It was 11 years later before a British newspaper published a crossword. The puzzle was immediately popular and now almost every newspaper publishes one.

A crossword designer follows these three rules.
- The grid is a square, with an odd number of rows and columns.
- Every answer has at least three letters.
- The pattern of black and white squares has **half-turn symmetry**. This means that the pattern is the same when the grid is turned 180° about its centre.

1 (a) Use the designer's rules.
 Copy and complete these crossword grids.
 Use tracing paper if you need to.

(b) For each crossword grid
- enter the clue numbers
- give the **total** number of clues.

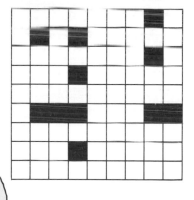

2 Design crossword grids to fit these descriptions.

Size of square	Number of black squares
5 by 5	6
7 by 7	12
7 by 7	13
9 by 9	14
9 by 9	15

3 Which square must always be black to give an odd number of black squares?

Ask your teacher what to do next.

Strangehill Secondary School

Pupils from five local primary schools go to Strangehill Secondary. Mrs Wong, the headmistress, drew this bar graph to show the number of first-year pupils from each school.

1 From what school did
(a) most (b) fewest pupils come?

2 (a) How many more pupils came from Croftbank than from Gladeside?
(b) Did more or fewer pupils come from Learnwell than from Parkland and Roseside together?
How many more or fewer?

3 (a) How many pupils in total came from the five schools?
(b) Strangehill had a first-year roll of 177. Give possible reasons why the number is different from your answer to part (a).

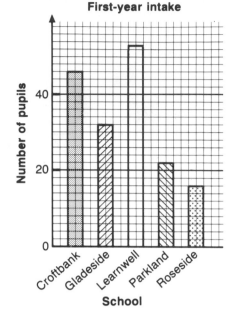

First-year intake

Pupil distribution

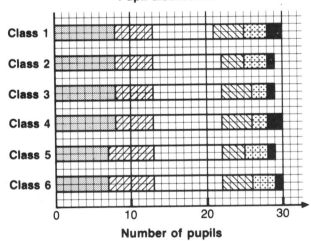

Number of pupils

There are six classes in the first year. The graph shows the distribution of pupils in each class.

4 Which classes have
(a) eight pupils from Croftbank
(b) only three pupils from Parkland
(c) more than five pupils from Gladeside?

5 What does the ■ shading show?

6 What do you notice about the way Mrs Wong has distributed the pupils?

7 Copy and complete the table.

		Number of pupils					
		Class					Total
	1	2	3	4	5	6	
Croftbank							
Gladeside	5	5	5	5	6	6	32
Learnwell							
Parkland							
Roseside							
Others							
Total		29					

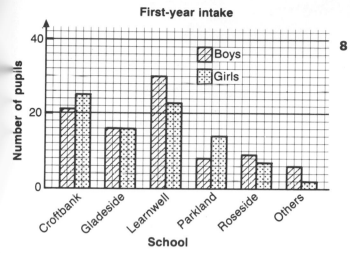

First-year intake

8 The bar graph shows the number of boys and girls from each school.
  (a) Look at the table below and the table in question **7**. Explain how Mrs Wong has allocated the pupils from Gladeside to classes.
  (b) Copy and complete the table below to show how **you** would allocate the other pupils to classes.

	Number of pupils															
	Class 1		Class 2		Class 3		Class 4		Class 5		Class 6		Total			
	Boys	Girls	Boys	Girls	Boys	Girls	Boys	Girls	Boys	Girls	Boys	Girls	Boys	Girls	Pupils
Croftbank															
Gladeside	3	2	3	2	2	3	2	3	3	3	3	3	16	16	32
Learnwell															
Parkland															
Roseside															
Others															
Total															

9 The graph shows the school roll of Strangehill Secondary from 1980 to 1990. How many
  (a) boys were on the roll in 1983
  (b) girls were on the roll in 1981
  (c) pupils were on the roll in 1987?

10 Which year had the fewest boys? How many boys were there then?

11 **(a)** In which year were there exactly 460 boys on the roll?
   (b) In which years was the number of girls less than 400?

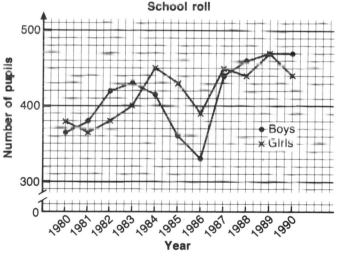

School roll

12 **(a)** In which year was the number of boys equal to the number of girls?
   (b) In which years were there more girls than boys?

13 Between 1985 and 1990 a large housing estate opened near Strangehill Secondary. In which year do you think the estate opened? Give reasons for your answer.

14 Between which years did **(a)** the number of boys on the school roll fall
   (b) the **total school roll** fall?

Ask your teacher what to do next.

Photographs

1 Use cm squared paper.
Mark is sticking these two photographs in an album. In each, the **total** of width and height is 10 cm.

4 cm

6 cm

6 cm

4 cm

(a) Draw all the possible sizes of rectangular photographs whose width and height have a total of 10 cm. Use only whole numbers.
(b) Inside each rectangle write its area.
(c) Give the width and height of the photograph with greatest area.

2 Leanne had this photograph on her bedroom wall. The width and height of the photograph are first-place decimals. They have
- a total of 1 $(0{\cdot}7 + 0{\cdot}3 = 1)$
- a product of 0·21 $(0{\cdot}7 \times 0{\cdot}3 = 0{\cdot}21)$

0·7

0·3

(a) Copy and complete the table to show the products (areas) for all possible pairs of first-place decimals (widths and heights) which total 1.
(b) Which pair of decimals has the greatest product?

First decimal (width)	Second decimal (height)	Total	Product (area)
0·7	0·3	1·0	0·21

0·8

1·2

3 Pierre is including this photograph in his new exhibition. Its width and height are first-place decimals which have a total of **2**.

(a) Which pair of first-place decimals which total 2 do you **think** gives the greatest product?
(b) Investigate. Write about what you discover.

4 Try question **3** again for a pair of first-place decimals which total **3**.

5 Explain how to find the pair of numbers which gives the greatest possible product when you only know their total.

Lengthwise

E11

Decimals 2:
Roots using
successive
approximations

1 What is the length of side of a square with **(a)** area 4 cm²
(b) area 9 cm²?

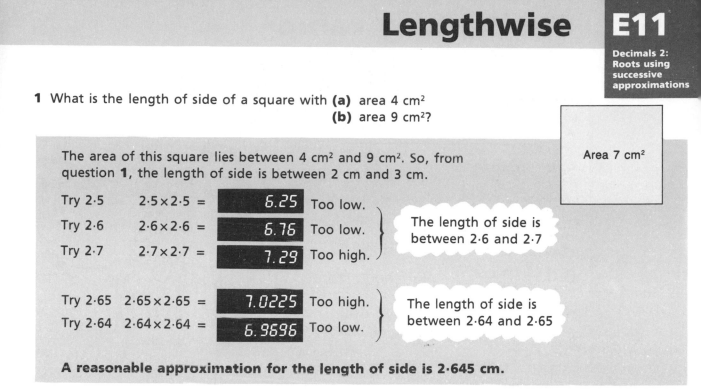

Area 7 cm²

The area of this square lies between 4 cm² and 9 cm². So, from question **1**, the length of side is between 2 cm and 3 cm.

Try 2·5	2·5 × 2·5 =	6.25	Too low.
Try 2·6	2·6 × 2·6 =	6.76	Too low.
Try 2·7	2·7 × 2·7 =	7.29	Too high.

The length of side is between 2·6 and 2·7

Try 2·65	2·65 × 2·65 =	7.0225	Too high.
Try 2·64	2·64 × 2·64 =	6.9696	Too low.

The length of side is between 2·64 and 2·65

A reasonable approximation for the length of side is 2·645 cm.

2 In the same way find the approximate length of side of a square with
(a) area 11 cm² **(b)** area 15 cm² **(c)** area 28 cm² **(d)** area 71 cm².

3 The length of side of the whole square is 16 cm.
(a) Calculate the area of the whole square.
(b) Find the area of the grey square.
(c) Find the length of side of the grey square.

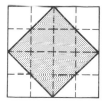

4 What is the length of edge of a cube with
(a) volume 8 cm³
(b) volume 27 cm³?

Volume 17 cm³

The volume of this cube lies between 8 cm³ and 27 cm³. So, from question **4**, the length of edge is between 2 cm and 3 cm.

Try 2·5	2·5 × 2·5 × 2·5 =	15.625	Too low.
Try 2·6	2·6 × 2·6 × 2·6 =	17.576	Too high.

The length of edge is between 2·5 and 2·6. It is nearer 2·6.

Try 2·56	2·56 × 2·56 × 2·56 =	16.777216	Too low.
Try 2·57	2·57 × 2·57 × 2·57 =	16.974593	Too low, but very close.
Try 2·58	2·58 × 2·58 × 2·58 =	17.173512	Too high.

The length of edge is between 2·57 and 2·58. It is nearer 2·57.

A reasonable approximation for the length of edge is 2·571 cm or 2·572 cm.

5 In the same way find the approximate length of edge of a cube with
(a) volume 24 cm³ **(b)** volume 41 cm³ **(c)** volume 79 cm³.

Ask your teacher what do to next.

Whole Day Excursions

SEA FISHING	Monday, Wednesday
WILDLIFE PARK	Monday, Thursday
GO-KARTING	Monday, Friday
CAVES	Tuesday, Thursday
BUTTERFLY KINGDOM	Tuesday, Friday
MARINE PARK	Wednesday, Friday

FREE Choose any three! FREE

Greg and Fiona are on holiday for a week.
The price includes three free excursions.

1 Greg chooses Sea fishing (S), Caves (C) and Marine park (M).
List all the possible ways he can plan his week. Start like this:

Greg

	Mon	Tues	Wed	Thur	Fri
Plan 1	S	C	M	✕	✕
Plan 2	S	C	✕	✕	M

2 Fiona chooses Wildlife park (W), Go-karting (G) and Butterfly
kingdom (B).
List all her possible plans.

3 Which plans leave both Greg and Fiona free to go to the
beach on Tuesday **and** Wednesday?

In the Airspeed Export Company's sales office engineers have to connect the computers to each other.

They need **1** line to connect **2** computers.

They need **3** lines to connect **3** computers.   They need **6** lines to connect **4** computers.

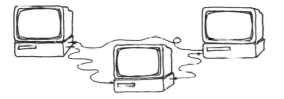   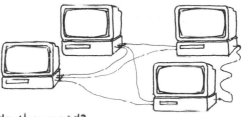

1 Draw a diagram for 5 computers. How many lines do they need?

2 Copy this table. Record the number of lines for 2, 3, 4 and 5 computers.

Number of computers	1	2	3	4	5	6	7	8
Number of lines	0							

3 (a) How many lines do you **think** they will need for 6 computers? Check by drawing a diagram.
(b) Complete your table.

4 The sales office of the Airspeed Export Company has 10 computers. How many lines do the engineers need to connect them to each other?

5 (a) Look at the diagram for 4 computers. How many lines are connected to **each** computer? How many lines are there altogether?
(b) Look at your diagram for 5 computers. How many lines are connected to **each** computer? How many lines are there altogether?
(c) Describe how to find the number of lines when you know the number of computers.

6 Use your rule. How many lines would you need to connect
(a) 12 computers   **(b)** 20 computers   **(c)** 50 computers?

7 (a) Use a 360° protractor. Draw round it and mark 12 equally spaced points on the circumference. Join each point to **every** other point.
(b) How many lines have you drawn? Explain your answer.

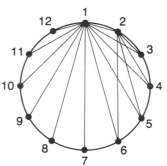

Ask your teacher what to do next.

Which day?

On 29 May 1953 Edmund Hillary and Tensing Norgay
became the first men to climb Mount Everest.
To find which day of the week they reached the
summit use the formula

$(D + M + Y) \div 7$ where D is the day of the month (1 to 31)

M is the **month code** (0 to 6)

Y is the **year code** (0 to 6)

The **remainder** gives the day of the week.

The tables below show the code for the day of the week, M and Y.

For **29 May 1953**

the day of the month is 29, $D = 29$

the month code is 2, $M = 2$

the year code is 3, $Y = 3$

$(D + M + Y) \div 7$
$= (29 + 2 + 3) \div 7$
$= 34 \div 7$
$= 4$ **remainder 6**

Mount Everest was first conquered on a Friday.

Remainder	Day
0	Sat
1	Sun
2	Mon
3	Tue
4	Wed
5	Thu
6	Fri

Month	Code (M)
Jan	1
Feb	4
Mar	4
Apr	0
May	2
Jun	5
Jul	0
Aug	3
Sep	6
Oct	1
Nov	4
Dec	6

In a **leap** year
subtract 1 from the
month code for Jan
and Feb.

Year	Code (Y)	Year	Code (Y)	Year	Code (Y)	Year	Code (Y)
1952	2	1953	3	1954	4	1955	5
1956	0	1957	1	1958	2	1959	3
1960	5	1961	6	1962	0	1963	1
1964	3	1965	4	1966	5	1967	6
1968	1	1969	2	1970	3	1971	4
1972	6	1973	0	1974	1	1975	2
1976	4	1977	5	1978	6	1979	0
1980	2	1981	3	1982	4	1983	5
1984	0	1985	1	1986	2	1987	3
1988	5	1989	6	1990	0	1991	1
1992	3	1993	4	1994	5	1995	6

1 Find what day of the week you were born.

2 Find what day of the week each of these events took place.
  (a) On 30 July 1966 England won the World Cup.
  (b) On 12 April 1961 Yuri Gagarin became the first man in space.
  (c) On 22 November 1963 President J. F. Kennedy was assassinated.
  (d) On 6 May 1954 Roger Bannister ran the first sub-4-minute mile.
  (e) On 20 July 1969 Neil Amstrong became the first man on the Moon.

3 Which day of the week was **(a)** New Year's day 1988 **(b)** St Valentine's day 1976?

Challenge

4 (a) On which day of the week will the year 2000 begin?
  (b) Find the Black Fridays, Friday the 13th, in 1990.

A **network** is made up of **points**, **regions** and **lines**.

These four networks
each have

4 points →
2 regions →
and 5 lines →

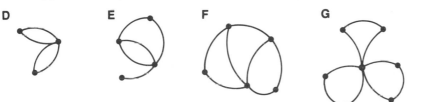
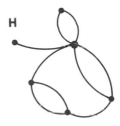

Lines only meet at points and do not cross.

1 (a) Copy and complete the table for these networks.

Network	Number of points (p)	Number of regions (r)	p + r	Number of lines (l)
D				
E				
F				
G				
H				

(b) Compare the last two columns in your table. What do
you notice?

(c) Copy and complete the formula:
number of points + number of regions = number of lines + ☐
p + r = l + ☐

2 (a) Use the formula. Copy and complete this table.

Network	p	r	l
V	2	2	
W	3	2	
X		3	6
Y	5		6
Z		4	8

(b) Draw networks for **V**, **W**, **X**, **Y** and **Z**.

3 Use the formula.
(a) Find p when $r = 6$ and $l = 8$.
(b) Find r when $p = 7$ and $l = 10$.
(c) Find l when $p = 5$ and $r = 8$.
(d) Find r when $p = 11$ and $l = 15$.

4 Draw networks for question **3**.

All the way round

1 Find the perimeter of each of these stamps.

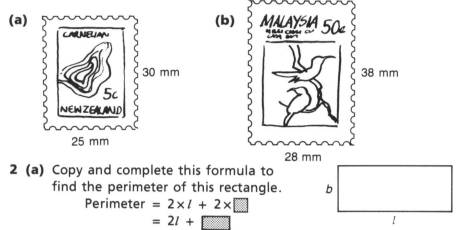

(a) 30 mm, 25 mm

(b) 38 mm, 28 mm

2 (a) Copy and complete this formula to
find the perimeter of this rectangle.

Perimeter = 2 × *l* + 2 × ▨

= 2*l* + ▨

b

l

(b) Check that the formula works for each stamp in question **1**.

3 Use the formula to find the perimeter of each of these stamps.

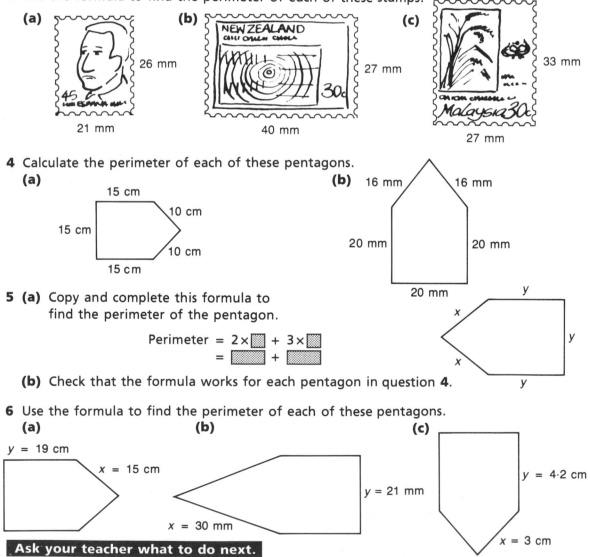

(a) 26 mm, 21 mm

(b) NEW ZEALAND — 27 mm, 40 mm

(c) 33 mm, 27 mm

4 Calculate the perimeter of each of these pentagons.

(a) 15 cm, 15 cm, 15 cm, 10 cm, 10 cm

(b) 16 mm, 16 mm, 20 mm, 20 mm, 20 mm

5 (a) Copy and complete this formula to
find the perimeter of the pentagon.

Perimeter = 2 × ▨ + 3 × ▨

= ▨ + ▨

x, *x*, *y*, *y*, *y*

(b) Check that the formula works for each pentagon in question **4**.

6 Use the formula to find the perimeter of each of these pentagons.

(a) *y* = 19 cm, *x* = 15 cm

(b) *x* = 30 mm, *y* = 21 mm

(c) *y* = 4·2 cm, *x* = 3 cm

Ask your teacher what to do next.

You need 2 mm squared paper.

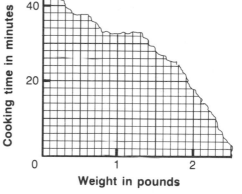

1 The table shows the approximate time
it takes to cook a chicken in a gas oven.

Weight in pounds (lb)	2	$3\frac{1}{2}$	5
Cooking time in minutes	60	90	120

(a) Draw axes using these scales:
Weight axis: **2 cm represents 1 pound.**
Time axis: **1 cm represents 10 minutes.**
(b) Plot the points and draw a straight line through them.

2 How long should it take to cook a chicken which weighs
(a) 3 lb (b) 4 lb (c) $2\frac{1}{2}$ lb (d) $4\frac{3}{4}$ lb?

3 (a) Chris puts a $2\frac{1}{2}$ lb chicken in the oven at 6.20 pm. When should it be ready?
(b) Carmel wants her $3\frac{1}{4}$ lb chicken to be cooked by 7.15 pm.
When should she put it in the oven?

4 This table shows the approximate time
it takes to cook a chicken in a
microwave oven.

Weight in pounds (lb)	2	$2\frac{1}{2}$	5
Cooking time in minutes	28	32	52

(a) Draw axes using these scales:
Weight axis: **2 cm represents 1 pound.**
Time axis: **1 cm represents 5 minutes.**
(b) Plot the points and draw a straight line
through them.

5 In a microwave oven, how long should it take to cook a
chicken which weighs
(a) 3 lb (b) 4 lb (c) $1\frac{1}{2}$ lb (d) $4\frac{3}{4}$ lb?

6 (a) How much time will Kelvin save by cooking a $4\frac{1}{2}$ lb
chicken in a microwave oven rather than in a gas oven?
(b) It takes 34 minutes to cook a chicken in a microwave
oven. How long should it take to cook this chicken in a
gas oven?

7 Copy and complete:
(a) For a **gas** oven,
cooking time = ▓ minutes per pound + ▓ minutes.
(b) For a **microwave** oven,
cooking time = ▓ minutes per pound + ▓ minutes.

Challenge

Emergency repairs

Dave has a burst pipe in his attic.
He needs a plumber.

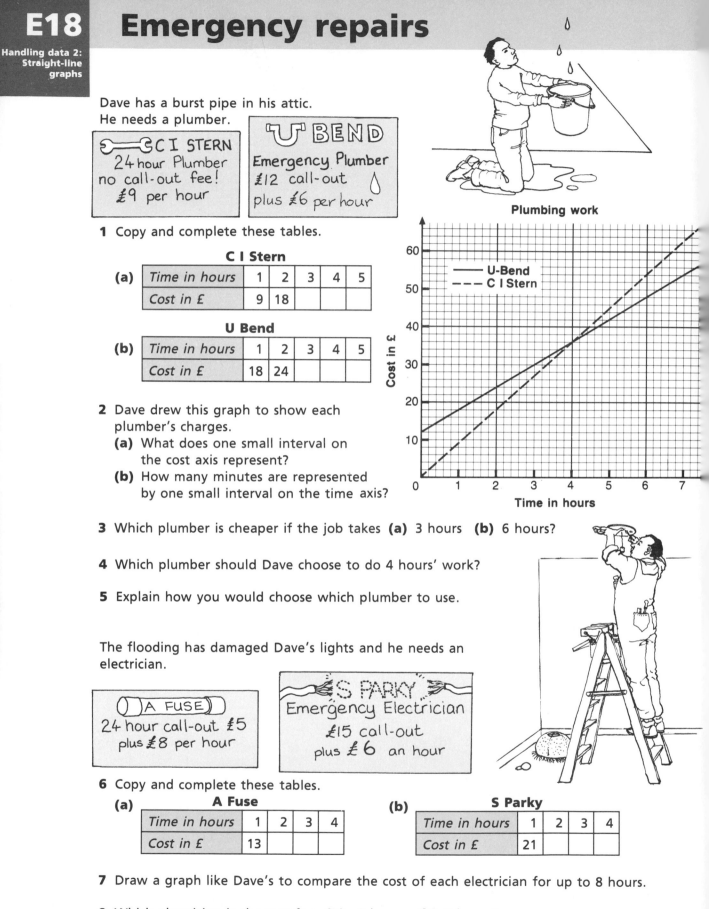

C I STERN
24 hour Plumber
no call-out fee!
£9 per hour

U BEND
Emergency Plumber
£12 call-out
plus £6 per hour

Plumbing work

1 Copy and complete these tables.

C I Stern

(a)
Time in hours	1	2	3	4	5
Cost in £	9	18			

U Bend

(b)
Time in hours	1	2	3	4	5
Cost in £	18	24			

2 Dave drew this graph to show each
plumber's charges.
(a) What does one small interval on
the cost axis represent?
(b) How many minutes are represented
by one small interval on the time axis?

3 Which plumber is cheaper if the job takes **(a)** 3 hours **(b)** 6 hours?

4 Which plumber should Dave choose to do 4 hours' work?

5 Explain how you would choose which plumber to use.

The flooding has damaged Dave's lights and he needs an
electrician.

A FUSE
24 hour call-out £5
plus £8 per hour

S PARKY
Emergency Electrician
£15 call-out
plus £6 an hour

6 Copy and complete these tables.

(a) **A Fuse**
Time in hours	1	2	3	4
Cost in £	13			

(b) **S Parky**
Time in hours	1	2	3	4
Cost in £	21			

7 Draw a graph like Dave's to compare the cost of each electrician for up to 8 hours.

8 Which electrician is cheaper for **(a)** 3 hours **(b)** 7 hours?

9 Explain how you would choose which electrician to use.

Leela used a small immersion heater to boil a beaker of water.
She drew a graph to show the change in temperature.

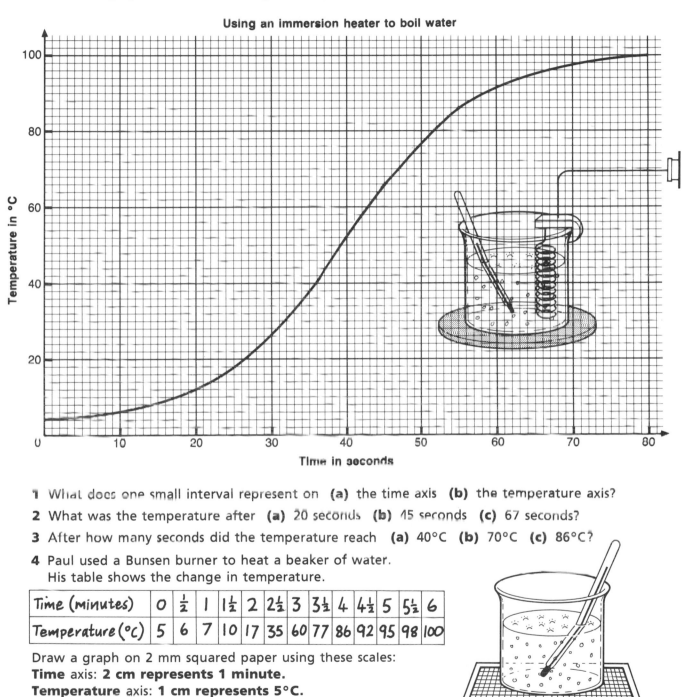

Using an immersion heater to boil water

1 What does one small interval represent on **(a)** the time axis **(b)** the temperature axis?

2 What was the temperature after **(a)** 20 seconds **(b)** 45 seconds **(c)** 67 seconds?

3 After how many seconds did the temperature reach **(a)** 40°C **(b)** 70°C **(c)** 86°C?

4 Paul used a Bunsen burner to heat a beaker of water.
His table shows the change in temperature.

Time (minutes)	0	½	1	1½	2	2½	3	3½	4	4½	5	5½	6
Temperature (°C)	5	6	7	10	17	35	60	77	86	92	95	98	100

Draw a graph on 2 mm squared paper using these scales:
Time axis: **2 cm represents 1 minute.**
Temperature axis: **1 cm represents 5°C.**

5 After how many minutes did the temperature reach
(a) 30°C **(b)** 65°C **(c)** 83°C?

6 How long did it take the temperature to increase fróm
(a) 10°C to 40°C **(b)** 40°C to 70°C **(c)** 70°C to 100°C?

Ask your teacher what to do next.

Movement patterns

You can make designs for decorations by moving shapes on a grid.

Sliding

1 (a) Mark off squared paper in 5 by 5 squares as shown.
   (b) Copy the design in the position shown here. Trace the design.
   (c) By sliding the tracing across ➡ or down ⬇ draw a pattern to fill the grid.
   (d) Colour the pattern.

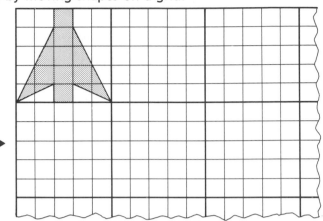

2 Use these designs, or some of your own, to make patterns by **sliding**.

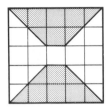 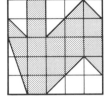 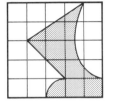

Turning over

3 (a) Mark off squared paper in 5 by 5 squares.
   (b) Draw this design in the top left corner. Trace the design.
   (c) Turn the tracing over ⬑ as shown. Trace the design.
   (d) Repeat until the first row is complete.

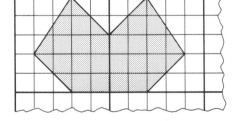

   (e) Start again in the top left corner.

   Turn the tracing over ⬐ as shown. Trace the design.
   (f) Repeat until the first column is complete.
   (g) By turning the tracing over ⬑ or ⬐ extend the pattern to fill the grid.

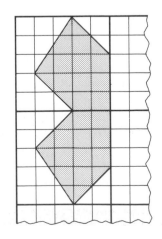

4 Use these designs, or some of your own, to make patterns by **turning over**.

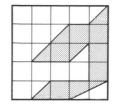
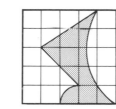
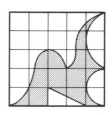

Sliding and turning over

5 This time,

● Do **not** mark off squared paper in larger squares.

● You can combine moves.

Try turning over ⤵ then

sliding down ↓ like this.

● Use designs of your own to make patterns by **sliding** and **turning over**.

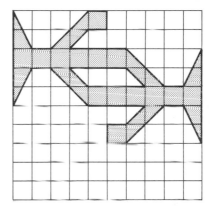

Ask your teacher what to do next.

Witches and wizards

At a meeting of witches and wizards there are 16 witches and 24 wizards.

1 Nine of the witches have broomsticks.
What fraction of the witches
(a) have a broomstick
(b) do not have a broomstick?

2 Eight of the wizards have wands.
What fraction of the wizards
(a) have a wand
(b) do not have a wand?

3 What fraction of those at the meeting are
(a) witches   (b) wizards?

4 Simplify each of these fractions.
(a) $\frac{5}{10}$ (b) $\frac{3}{12}$ (c) $\frac{2}{10}$ (d) $\frac{3}{6}$ (e) $\frac{6}{8}$ (f) $\frac{4}{6}$ (g) $\frac{6}{9}$ (h) $\frac{15}{25}$
(i) $\frac{15}{30}$ (j) $\frac{60}{100}$ (k) $\frac{12}{60}$ (l) $\frac{15}{60}$ (m) $\frac{12}{36}$ (n) $\frac{24}{36}$ (o) $\frac{14}{28}$ (p) $\frac{30}{75}$

5 *The Book of Magic* has 120 pages.
What fraction of the book is about
(a) spells   (b) potions   (c) tricks?

Willie Wizard spent £5 altogether on the ingredients for a magic potion. He spent 60p on green gunge.
What fraction of the £5 is this?

$$\frac{60p}{£5} = \frac{60}{500} = \frac{6}{50} = \frac{3}{25}$$

He spent $\frac{3}{25}$ of the £5 on green gunge.

6 For the other ingredients Willie spent
£2·75 on secret juice, 45p on
sludge and £1·20 on super-squidge.
What fraction of his £5 did he spend on
(a) secret juice   (b) sludge   (c) super-squidge?

7 In simplest form, what fraction is
(a) £1·30 of £2   (b) £1·75 of £3
(c) £1·60 of £2·40   (d) £1·40 of £4·20?

8 Two cloaks are made from a strip of cloth 4 m long. A wizard's cloak
needs 2 m 25 cm of cloth and the rest of the strip is used for a witch's
cloak. What fraction of the strip of cloth is needed to make
(a) a wizard's cloak   (b) a witch's cloak?

9 In simplest form, what fraction is
(a) 1 m 20 cm of 3 m
(b) 2 m 50 cm of 4 m
(c) 1 m 60 cm of 2 m
(d) 2 m 40 cm of 4 m 20 cm?

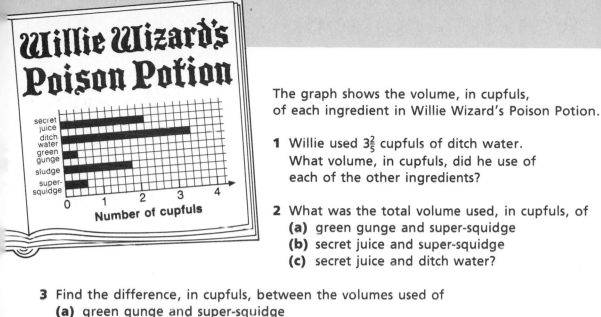

Willie Wizard's Poison Potion

The graph shows the volume, in cupfuls, of each ingredient in Willie Wizard's Poison Potion.

1 Willie used $3\frac{2}{5}$ cupfuls of ditch water.
What volume, in cupfuls, did he use of each of the other ingredients?

2 What was the total volume used, in cupfuls, of
  (a) green gunge and super-squidge
  (b) secret juice and super-squidge
  (c) secret juice and ditch water?

3 Find the difference, in cupfuls, between the volumes used of
  (a) green gunge and super-squidge
  (b) green gunge and sludge
  (c) secret juice and ditch water.

4 (a) $\frac{3}{10}+\frac{5}{10}$ **(b)** $\frac{3}{6}+2\frac{1}{6}$ **(c)** $2\frac{3}{20}+1\frac{7}{20}$ **(d)** $\frac{7}{8}-\frac{5}{8}$ **(e)** $4\frac{13}{25}-\frac{8}{25}$ **(f)** $4\frac{23}{100}-1\frac{13}{100}$

What was the total volume, in cupfuls, of ditch water and sludge used in the Poison Potion?

$$3\frac{2}{5}+1\frac{4}{5}$$
$$= 4\frac{6}{5}$$
$$= 5\frac{1}{5}$$
$\frac{6}{5}$ is $1\frac{1}{5}$
4 and $1\frac{1}{5}$ is $5\frac{1}{5}$
$5\frac{1}{5}$ cupfuls were used.

5 (a) $\frac{2}{5}+\frac{4}{5}$ **(b)** $\frac{5}{8}+\frac{6}{8}$ **(c)** $3\frac{2}{3}+\frac{2}{3}$
(d) $\frac{3}{5}+2\frac{4}{5}$ **(e)** $\frac{3}{6}+\frac{5}{6}$ **(f)** $1\frac{5}{8}+\frac{7}{8}$
(g) $2\frac{9}{10}+3\frac{3}{10}$ **(h)** $3\frac{3}{8}+1\frac{5}{8}$ **(i)** $\frac{5}{16}+4\frac{4}{16}$

$$2\frac{2}{5} = 1+1\frac{2}{5}$$
$$= 1+\frac{7}{5}$$
$$= 1\frac{7}{5}$$

6 Exchange 1 whole in each of these.
  (a) $2\frac{3}{5}$ **(b)** $3\frac{5}{8}$ **(c)** $4\frac{7}{8}$ **(d)** $2\frac{1}{3}$ **(e)** $4\frac{2}{3}$
  (f) $2\frac{3}{6}$ **(g)** $3\frac{3}{10}$ **(h)** $5\frac{3}{4}$ **(i)** $4\frac{7}{12}$ **(j)** $1\frac{1}{10}$

In cupfuls, how much more ditch water than sludge was used in Willie's potion?

$$2\frac{2}{5} = 1+1\frac{2}{5}$$
$$= 1+\frac{7}{5}$$
$$= 1\frac{7}{5}$$

$$3\frac{2}{5}-1\frac{4}{5}$$
$$= 2\frac{2}{5}-\frac{4}{5}$$
$$= 1\frac{7}{5}-\frac{4}{5}$$
$$=1\frac{3}{5}$$

$1\frac{3}{5}$ more cupfuls were used.

7 (a) $3\frac{1}{3}-\frac{2}{3}$ **(b)** $4\frac{2}{5}-\frac{4}{5}$
  (c) $2\frac{4}{8}-\frac{7}{8}$ **(d)** $4\frac{1}{3}-1\frac{2}{3}$
  (e) $3\frac{1}{5}-1\frac{3}{5}$ **(f)** $5\frac{3}{10}-1\frac{9}{10}$
  (g) $4\frac{5}{6}-2\frac{1}{6}$ **(h)** $3\frac{3}{10}-1\frac{7}{10}$
  (i) $5\frac{1}{8}-2\frac{3}{8}$ **(j)** $2\frac{3}{5}-1\frac{4}{5}$
  (k) $4\frac{3}{8}-3\frac{5}{8}$ **(l)** $4\frac{3}{20}-1\frac{19}{20}$

8 At 11 pm the temperature of Willie's Poison Potion was $93\frac{3}{5}$°C.
What was the temperature at
(a) 11.30 pm **(b)** midnight?

9 By how much, in °C, did the temperature rise between
(a) 11 pm and 11.30 pm
(b) 11.30 pm and midnight?

10 By 1 am the temperature had risen by another $2\frac{3}{5}$°C.
What was the temperature then?

11 pm

11.30 pm

Midnight

Mandy's pie shop

Mandy bakes and sells pies.
How much strawberry pie had she left on
Monday?
She had $\frac{3}{4}$ of one pie and $\frac{5}{8}$ of another pie left.

On Monday she had **$1\frac{3}{8}$** strawberry pies left.

$\frac{3}{4}+\frac{5}{8}$

$=\frac{6}{8}+\frac{5}{8}$

$=\frac{11}{8}$

$=\mathbf{1\frac{3}{8}}$

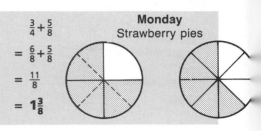

Monday
Strawberry pies

1 Find how much of each type of pie Mandy had left each day.

	Strawberry	Apple	Plum	Rhubarb
Monday	$\frac{3}{4}+\frac{5}{8}$	$\frac{1}{3}+1\frac{1}{6}$	$1\frac{5}{8}+\frac{3}{4}$	$\frac{2}{5}+\frac{3}{10}$
Tuesday	$1\frac{1}{4}+\frac{3}{8}$	$1\frac{5}{6}+\frac{2}{3}$	$\frac{1}{2}+1\frac{7}{8}$	$1\frac{3}{5}+1\frac{7}{10}$
Wednesday	$1\frac{5}{8}+1\frac{1}{2}$	$1\frac{2}{3}+\frac{5}{6}$	$1\frac{1}{4}+1\frac{3}{8}$	$1\frac{1}{2}+\frac{9}{10}$
Thursday	$\frac{7}{8}+1\frac{3}{4}$	$\frac{2}{3}+\frac{7}{12}$	$1\frac{3}{4}+\frac{7}{8}$	$\frac{4}{5}+1\frac{3}{10}$
Friday	$1\frac{3}{4}+2\frac{3}{8}$	$\frac{5}{6}+\frac{11}{12}$	$2\frac{1}{2}+1\frac{5}{8}$	$\frac{3}{5}+2\frac{9}{10}$

On Wednesday Mandy started with $5\frac{1}{3}$ plum pies.
At the end of the day she had $2\frac{5}{6}$ plum pies left.
How many had she sold?

$5\frac{1}{3} \quad -2\frac{5}{6}$

$=3\frac{1}{3} \quad -\frac{5}{6}$

$3\frac{2}{6} = 2+1\frac{2}{6} \qquad =3\frac{2}{6} \quad -\frac{5}{6}$

$\qquad\qquad =2+\frac{8}{6} \qquad =2\frac{8}{6} \quad -\frac{5}{6}$

$\qquad\qquad =2\frac{8}{6} \qquad\qquad =2\frac{3}{6}$

$\qquad\qquad\qquad\qquad\qquad =\mathbf{2\frac{1}{2}}$

She has sold **$2\frac{1}{2}$** plum pies.

2 The table shows the number of each type of pie at the start of each day.
The number **left** on Monday is the **starting** number for Tuesday.
Find how many of each type were sold on
(a) Monday **(b)** Tuesday **(c)** Wednesday.

	Strawberry	Apple	Plum	Rhubarb
Monday	10	10	10	10
Tuesday	$7\frac{3}{4}$	$6\frac{3}{10}$	$8\frac{7}{12}$	$8\frac{1}{4}$
Wednesday	$5\frac{1}{8}$	$3\frac{2}{5}$	$5\frac{1}{3}$	$5\frac{7}{12}$
Thursday	$\frac{3}{4}$	$1\frac{7}{10}$	$2\frac{5}{6}$	$1\frac{5}{6}$

3 (a) $3\frac{3}{4}+2\frac{1}{8}$ **(b)** $2\frac{2}{3}-1\frac{1}{6}$ **(c)** $4\frac{2}{5}+3\frac{7}{10}$ **(d)** $5\frac{4}{5}-2\frac{3}{10}$ **(e)** $2\frac{1}{2}+1\frac{5}{8}$

(f) $4\frac{1}{3}-1\frac{5}{6}$ **(g)** $3\frac{3}{4}+4\frac{7}{12}$ **(h)** $2\frac{1}{5}-\frac{9}{10}$ **(i)** $4\frac{2}{3}+5\frac{5}{6}$ **(j)** $3\frac{1}{12}-1\frac{3}{4}$

Ask your teacher what to do next.

To find the decimal form of a fraction, divide the numerator by the denominator.

numerator → $\frac{1}{4}$

denominator →

$$\frac{1}{4} = 1 \div 4 = 0.25 \qquad 4\overline{)1.00}^{\,0.25}$$

1 Find the decimal form of **(a)** $\frac{1}{2}$ **(b)** $\frac{1}{5}$ **(c)** $\frac{1}{10}$ **(d)** $\frac{1}{20}$ **(e)** $\frac{1}{8}$

2 The graph shows fractions, with **numerator 1**, in decimal form.
The arrows show that $\frac{1}{8}$ has decimal form 0·125.
Check your answers to question **1** by reading from the graph.

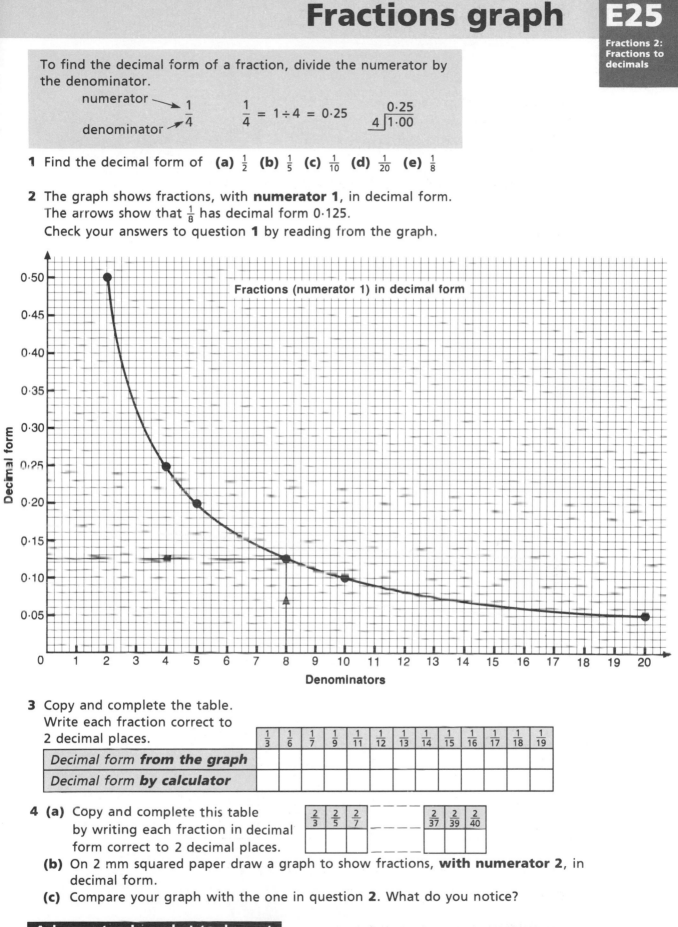

Fractions (numerator 1) in decimal form

Decimal form — vertical axis: 0·05, 0·10, 0·15, 0·20, 0·25, 0·30, 0·35, 0·40, 0·45, 0·50

Denominators — horizontal axis: 0 to 20

3 Copy and complete the table.
Write each fraction correct to 2 decimal places.

	$\frac{1}{3}$	$\frac{1}{6}$	$\frac{1}{7}$	$\frac{1}{9}$	$\frac{1}{11}$	$\frac{1}{12}$	$\frac{1}{13}$	$\frac{1}{14}$	$\frac{1}{15}$	$\frac{1}{16}$	$\frac{1}{17}$	$\frac{1}{18}$	$\frac{1}{19}$
Decimal form **from the graph**													
Decimal form **by calculator**													

4 (a) Copy and complete this table
by writing each fraction in decimal
form correct to 2 decimal places.

$\frac{2}{3}$	$\frac{2}{5}$	$\frac{2}{7}$	– – –	$\frac{2}{37}$	$\frac{2}{39}$	$\frac{2}{40}$

(b) On 2 mm squared paper draw a graph to show fractions, **with numerator 2**, in decimal form.

(c) Compare your graph with the one in question **2**. What do you notice?

Ask your teacher what to do next.

New prices

The Goodies catalogue is having a price review.

The price of the radio is to be **increased by 8%**.
The new price is **108% of £27**.
To find the new price

Enter **1.08** Press **×** **2** **7** **=** to give **29.16**

or Enter **27.** Press **×** **1** **0** **8** **%** to give **29.16**

The new price is **£29·16**.

£27

1 The catalogue is making the following
price increases: radios 8%, personal
stereos 12%, cameras 16%.

Find the new price
of each item.

£32 **Q**

PERSONAL
STEREOS   **P** RADIO   £34

£84
S

CAMERAS   **T** £60

£20

R

In a sale the price of a frying pan was
reduced by 5%.

The sale price is **95% of £12**.

To find the sale price

Enter **0.95** Press **×** **1** **2** **=** to give **11.4**

or Enter **12.** Press **×** **9** **5** **%** to give **11.4**

The sale price is **£11·40**.

Magic Frying Pan
Used by chefs everywhere.

5% OFF

SALE
Was £12
Now Only   £11·40

2 Find the **sale price** for items **A** to **F**.

SALE   Toys 15% OFF   Calculators 9% OFF

Clothes 12% OFF

SALE

A **Supawarm Windproof Jacket**
Cosy wrap for a cold snap
Was **£38** – Now Only

B **Building Bricks**
The best bricks for children
Was **£13** – Now Only

C **The Basicalc**
The calculator you can count on.
Was **£5** – Now Only

D **Scientific Calculator**
All the answers at your fingertips.
Was **£15** – Now Only

E **Rock 'n' Roll Tee Shirt**
To fit boys and girls – unisex
Was **£6** – Now Only

F **The Wanda-Doll**
Can bend to any shape.
Amuses children for hours.
Was **£26** – Now Only

Wanda

`0.3481625` can be written as 0·35 to the nearest hundredth.
0·35 = 35 hundredths or 35%

`0.3481625` is about 35%

1 Write each of these decimals to the nearest hundredth and as a percentage:

(a) `0.2741561`   (b) `0.67852`   (c) `0.116558`   (d) `0.9225`   (e) `0.5186`

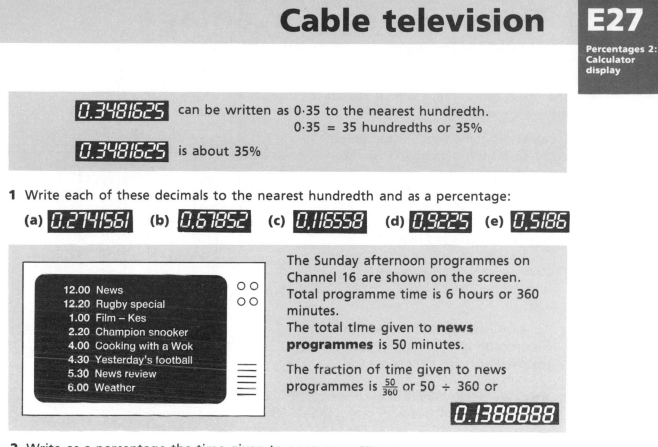

The Sunday afternoon programmes on Channel 16 are shown on the screen.
Total programme time is 6 hours or 360 minutes.
The total time given to **news programmes** is 50 minutes.

The fraction of time given to news programmes is $\frac{50}{360}$ or 50 ÷ 360 or

`0.1388888`

Programme listing:
12.00 News
12.20 Rugby special
1.00 Film – Kes
2.20 Champion snooker
4.00 Cooking with a Wok
4.30 Yesterday's football
5.30 News review
6.00 Weather

2 Write as a percentage the time given to news programmes.

3 During the afternoon, advertisements take up 55 minutes.
What percentage of the 6 hours is this?

4 Calculate the percentage of time given to **(a)** the film **(b)** sport.

Channel 18 carried out a survey. They asked 520 viewers these two questions:

'Should there be a separate channel for sport?'   'Should Channel 10 show advertisements?'

The screens show the results.

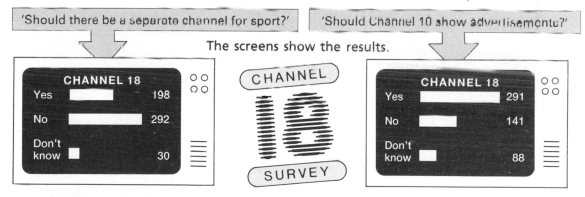

CHANNEL 18
Yes   198
No   292
Don't know   30

CHANNEL 18 SURVEY

CHANNEL 18
Yes   291
No   141
Don't know   88

5 In the question about 'a separate channel for sport', what percentage of the viewers replied
(a) Yes **(b)** No **(c)** Don't know?

6 Repeat question **5** for the replies about advertisements.

7 Work as a group.
   (a) Carry out your own survey for a TV channel. Ask as many pupils as possible the same two questions as those above. Express your results as percentages.
   (b) Compare your percentage results with those for Channel 18.

The smoking percentage

The graph shows the results of annual surveys on smoking.

1 (a) What is the trend of the graph?
  (b) Is this trend what you would expect? Explain.

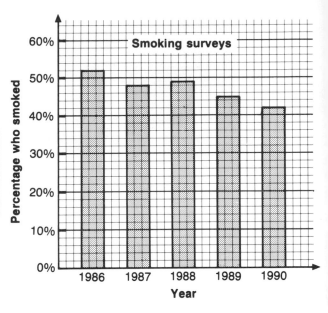

In the 1986 survey the percentage of people who smoked was 52%.
The fraction of people who smoked was $\frac{52}{100} = \frac{13}{25}$

2 For each year find, in simplest form, the fraction of people surveyed who
(a) smoked **(b)** did not smoke.

3 There were 500 people in each survey. For each year write the number of people who **(a)** smoked **(b)** did not smoke.

4 Use your answers to question **3**.
Copy and complete the table.

	Number of smokers in				
	1986	1987	1988	1989	1990
Male	168	146		129	
Female			93		97
Total	260				

In the 1986 survey the fraction of smokers who were male was
$\frac{168}{260} = 168 \div 260$
$= 0.6461538$ which is about **65%**.

5 For each survey find the percentage of smokers who were
(a) male **(b)** female.

6 In each survey there were equal numbers of men and women.
Find for each year
(a) the percentage of males who smoked
(b) the percentage of females who smoked.

7 Work as a group.
(a) Draw graphs to illustrate your answers to questions **5** and **6**.
(b) Write about your graphs.

Investigation

8 Carry out a survey of your own.

Ask your teacher what to do next.

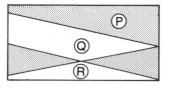

Eric uses rectangles to design coloured panels.

He has divided this rectangle into regions. He has coloured it using these rules:
● regions sharing a boundary, like Ⓟ and Ⓠ, **must** have different colours.
● regions which meet only at a point, like Ⓠ and Ⓡ, **may** have the same colour.

1 Copy these rectangles and use Eric's rules to colour the regions using as **few** colours as possible. Write the number of colours **needed** for each rectangle.

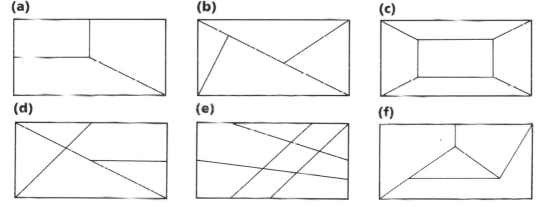

(a)   **(b)**   **(c)**

(d)   **(e)**   **(f)**

2 (a) Using Eric's rules, design and colour some rectangles of your own.

(b) How many different colours are **needed** to colour a rectangle of any design?

Eric's new range uses rectangles divided into regions by drawing straight lines from **edge to edge**.

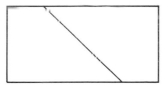

3 or 4 → regions

1 line makes 2 regions.   2 lines make a **maximum** of 4 regions.

3 Find the maximum number of regions Eric can make by drawing **(a)** 3 lines **(b)** 4 lines.

4 (a) Copy and complete the table.
(b) Describe the pattern in your table.
(c) What do you **think** the maximum number of regions is for 5 lines?

Number of lines	1	2	3	4
Maximum number of regions				11

(d) Check your answer to part **(c)** by drawing. Were you correct?
(e) Discuss how to draw the lines to give the maximum number of regions.

5 Colour each of your rectangles in the same way as those in question **1**. What do you notice?

Ask your teacher what to do next.

Polygons

Joanne is investigating polygons for counter shapes in a new game.

A polygon is a flat shape with all its sides straight.

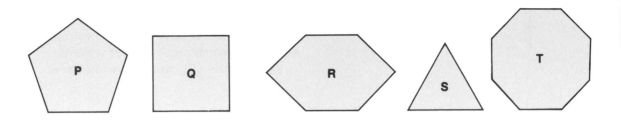

1 (a) For each polygon **P**, **Q**, **R**, **S** and **T** write the number of
sides **and** the number of angles.
(b) A polygon has 12 sides. How many angles does it have?

2 A **regular** polygon has all its sides the same length and all its
angles the same size.
(a) Which of the shapes **P**, **Q,**, **R**, **S** and **T**, do you **think** are
regular polygons?
(b) Make a tracing of each polygon. Rotate your tracings.
Which of the shapes **are** regular polygons?
(c) What is the name of a regular polygon with
● 3 sides ● 4 sides ● 5 sides?

A regular pentagon can be divided into
congruent (identical) triangles as shown.

The sum of the 5 marked angles is 360°.

The size of each marked angle is
360° ÷ 5 = **72°**.

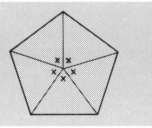

3 Find the size of the marked angles in each of these regular polygons.

(a)

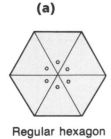

Regular hexagon

(b)

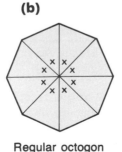

Regular octogon

(c)

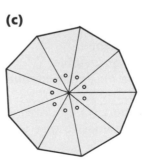

Regular nonagon

(d)

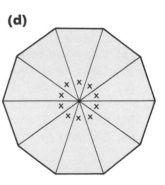

Regular decagon

Regular polygons

E31

Angles 2:
Constructing
regular
polygons

1 Follow these steps to draw a regular pentagon.

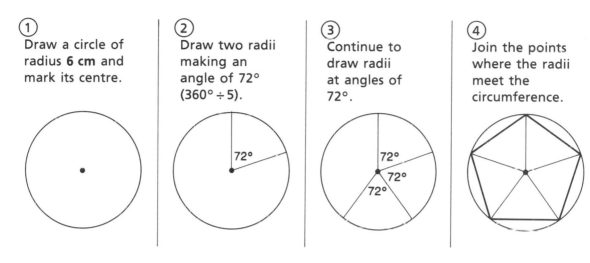

① Draw a circle of radius **6 cm** and mark its centre.

② Draw two radii making an angle of 72° (360° ÷ 5).

72°

③ Continue to draw radii at angles of 72°.

72°
72°
72°

④ Join the points where the radii meet the circumference.

2 Use this method to draw a regular nonagon.

3 Draw **(a)** a regular hexagon
(b) a regular octagon.

Hint:
Draw diameters
instead of radii.

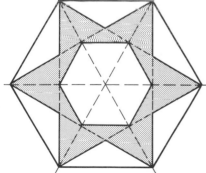

4 Use the regular polygons you have drawn. Make and colour designs like these.

5 Draw an enlargement of the shape of a 50 pence coin.

Challenge

Ask your teacher what to do next.

Tom, Ally, Sue and
Rehana are looking at a
mystic cube.
Here is the cube split
into layers.

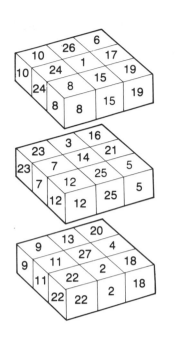

1 This is the face that Tom
sees.

10	24	8
23	7	12
9	11	22

Draw the faces that Ally,
Sue and Rehana see.

2 (a) For each face, add up each row and each column.
What do you notice?

(b) Find the sum for the diagonals. What do you notice?

3 Here are the
layers of another
mystic cube.
Draw all six faces
of the cube and
find the missing
numbers.

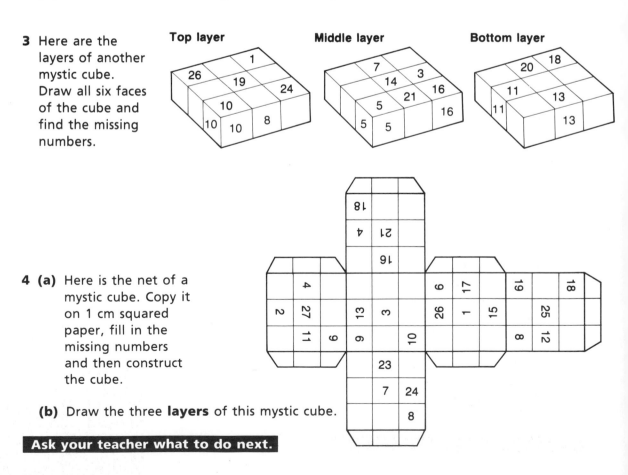

4 (a) Here is the net of a
mystic cube. Copy it
on 1 cm squared
paper, fill in the
missing numbers
and then construct
the cube.

(b) Draw the three **layers** of this mystic cube.

Ask your teacher what to do next.

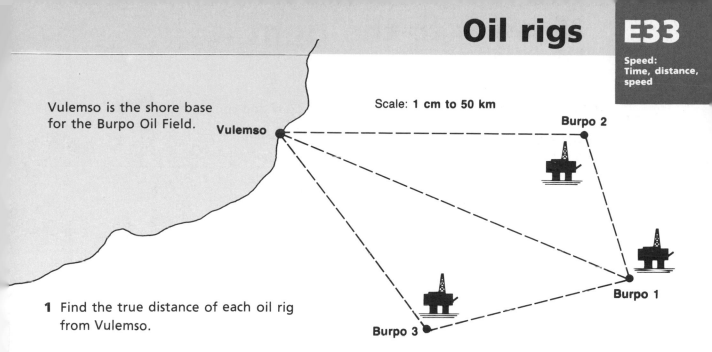

Vulemso is the shore base
for the Burpo Oil Field.

Scale: 1 cm to 50 km

1 Find the true distance of each oil rig
from Vulemso.

2 A supply vessel can sail at 20 kilometres per hour. Copy and complete this table.

Speed 20 km/h	Time	$\frac{1}{2}$ hour	1 hour	2 hours	5 hours	7 hours
	Distance		20 km			

3 How long should it take the supply vessel to sail from Vulemso to
(a) Burpo 1 **(b)** Burpo 2?

4 (a) How far is it from Burpo 1 to Burpo 2?
(b) How long should the supply vessel take to sail from Burpo 1 to Burpo 2?

5 A helicopter can fly at 150 kilometres per hour. Copy and complete this table.

Speed 150 km/h	Time	1 hour	2 hours	3 hours	4 hours	6 hours
	Distance	150 km				

6 How many minutes should it take the helicopter to fly
(a) 75 kilometres **(b)** 50 kilometres **(c)** 25 kilometres?

7 How long should it take the helicopter to fly from Vulemso to
(a) Burpo 1 **(b)** Burpo 2 **(c)** Burpo 3
(d) Burpo 1, then to Burpo 2, then back to Vulemso?

8 (a) The helicopter leaves Vulemso at
0615 on Tuesdays to visit the oil
rigs. It stops for three hours at
each oil rig and then flies back to
Vulemso. At what time should it
arrive back at Vulemso?
(b) Repeat question **8(a)** for the supply
vessel which leaves Vulemso at
0800 on Mondays and stops for
10 hours at each oil rig.

Ask your teacher what to do next.

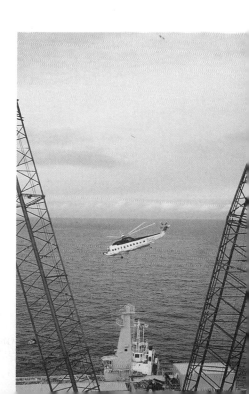

Move it to the right . . .

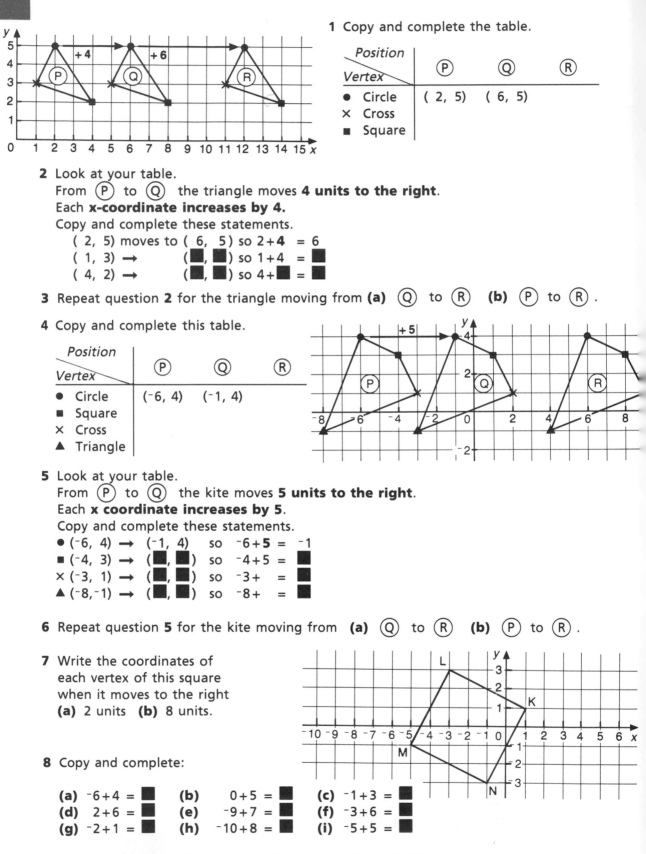

1 Copy and complete the table.

Position Vertex	(P)	(Q)	(R)
● Circle	(2, 5)	(6, 5)	
✕ Cross			
■ Square			

2 Look at your table.
From (P) to (Q) the triangle moves **4 units to the right**.
Each **x-coordinate increases by 4.**
Copy and complete these statements.
    (2, 5) moves to (6, 5) so 2+**4** = 6
    (1, 3) →   (■, ■) so 1+4 = ■
    (4, 2) →   (■, ■) so 4+■ = ■

3 Repeat question **2** for the triangle moving from **(a)** (Q) to (R)   **(b)** (P) to (R) .

4 Copy and complete this table.

Position Vertex	(P)	(Q)	(R)
● Circle	(⁻6, 4)	(⁻1, 4)	
■ Square			
✕ Cross			
▲ Triangle			

5 Look at your table.
From (P) to (Q) the kite moves **5 units to the right**.
Each **x coordinate increases by 5**.
Copy and complete these statements.
  ● (⁻6, 4) → (⁻1, 4)   so ⁻6+**5** = ⁻1
  ■ (⁻4, 3) → (■, ■) so ⁻4+5 = ■
  ✕ (⁻3, 1) → (■, ■) so ⁻3+ = ■
  ▲ (⁻8,⁻1) → (■, ■) so ⁻8+ = ■

6 Repeat question **5** for the kite moving from **(a)** (Q) to (R)   **(b)** (P) to (R) .

7 Write the coordinates of
each vertex of this square
when it moves to the right
(a) 2 units **(b)** 8 units.

8 Copy and complete:

  (a) ⁻6+4 = ■   **(b)**   0+5 = ■   **(c)** ⁻1+3 = ■
  (d) 2+6 = ■   **(e)** ⁻9+7 = ■   **(f)** ⁻3+6 = ■
  (g) ⁻2+1 = ■   **(h)** ⁻10+8 = ■   **(i)** ⁻5+5 = ■

9 A triangle has coordinates R(3, 2), S(⁻7,⁻3), T(⁻2, 4). Without drawing a diagram
write the new coordinates when it is moved **to the right**
  (a) 3 units **(b)** 12 units **(c)** 20 units.

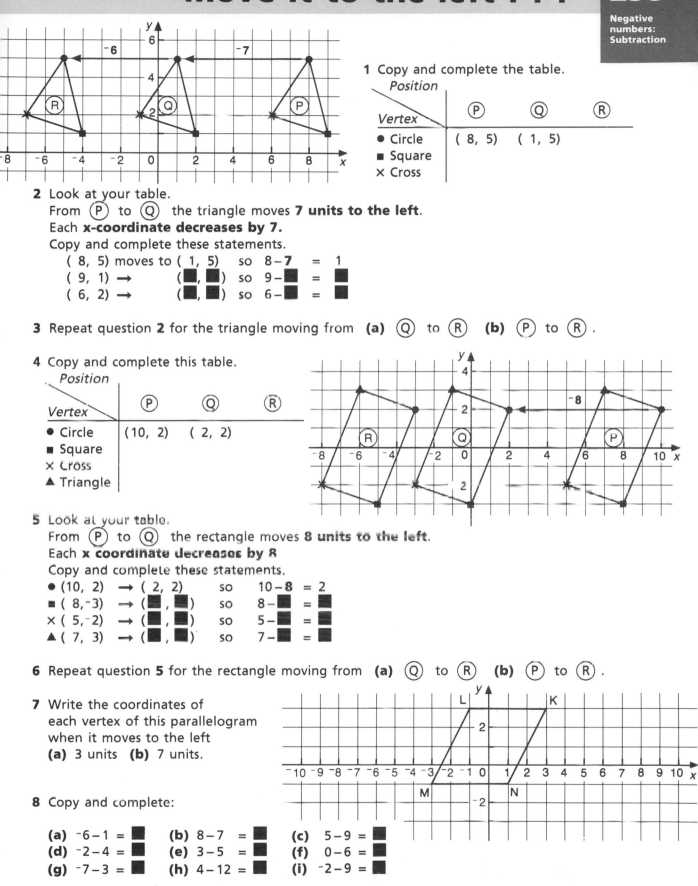

1 Copy and complete the table.

Position Vertex	(P)	(Q)	(R)
● Circle	(8, 5)	(1, 5)	
■ Square			
✕ Cross			

2 Look at your table.
From (P) to (Q) the triangle moves **7 units to the left**.
Each **x-coordinate decreases by 7.**
Copy and complete these statements.

(8, 5) moves to (1, 5)   so   8 – **7** = 1
(9, 1) → (■, ■)   so   9 – ■ = ■
(6, 2) → (■, ■)   so   6 – ■ = ■

3 Repeat question **2** for the triangle moving from **(a)** (Q) to (R) **(b)** (P) to (R).

4 Copy and complete this table.

Position Vertex	(P)	(Q)	(R)
● Circle	(10, 2)	(2, 2)	
■ Square			
✕ Cross			
▲ Triangle			

5 Look at your table.
From (P) to (Q) the rectangle moves **8 units to the left**.
Each **x coordinate decreases by 8**
Copy and complete these statements.

● (10, 2) → (2, 2)   so   10 – **8** = 2
■ (8, ⁻3) → (■, ■)   so   8 – ■ = ■
✕ (5, ⁻2) → (■, ■)   so   5 – ■ = ■
▲ (7, 3) → (■, ■)   so   7 – ■ = ■

6 Repeat question **5** for the rectangle moving from **(a)** (Q) to (R) **(b)** (P) to (R).

7 Write the coordinates of
each vertex of this parallelogram
when it moves to the left
(a) 3 units **(b)** 7 units.

8 Copy and complete:

(a) ⁻6 – 1 = ■   **(b)** 8 – 7 = ■   **(c)** 5 – 9 = ■
(d) ⁻2 – 4 = ■   **(e)** 3 – 5 = ■   **(f)** 0 – 6 = ■
(g) ⁻7 – 3 = ■   **(h)** 4 – 12 = ■   **(i)** ⁻2 – 9 = ■

9 A triangle has coordinates R(⁻4, 1), S(⁻1, ⁻3), T(2, 5). Without drawing a diagram
write the new coordinates when it moves
(a) 2 units to the **left** **(b)** 15 units to the **left** **(c)** 15 units to the **right**.

At midnight the temperature was $x°$C. By noon it had risen by 12°C to 8°C.

To find the unknown temperature:
- Form an equation. → $x + 12 = 8$
- Solve it. → $x = {}^-4$

At midnight the temperature was **${}^-4$°C**.

$? + 12 = 8$
${}^-4 + 12 = 8$

1 For each of the following **form an equation** and solve it to find the unknown temperature.

(a) At midnight the temperature was $x°$C. By sunrise it had risen by 5 degrees to 3°C.

(b) The temperature in Cardiff at noon was $g°$C. In Benidorm it was 17 degrees higher at 12°C.

(c) On Christmas day the highest temperature in Manchester was $n°$C. Six months later it was 31 degrees higher at 24°C.

(d) The temperature in the cold store was $w°$C. Outside the building it was 29 degrees higher at 23°C.

(e) In Siberia the temperature was $t°$C. At the same time in Belfast it was 25 degrees higher at ${}^-2$°C.

In the desert the highest daytime temperature was $d°$C. During the night it fell by 43 degrees to ${}^-5$°C.

To find the unknown temperature:

- Form an equation. → $d - 43 = {}^-5$
- Solve it. → $d = 38$

The highest daytime temperature was **38°C**.

$? - 43 = {}^-5$
$38 - 43 = {}^-5$

2 For each of the following **form an equation** and solve it to find the unknown temperature.

(a) The temperature in the kitchen was $f°$C. The temperature inside the freezer was 25 degrees lower at ${}^-8$°C.

(b) The temperature in the basket of a hot-air balloon was $b°$C. As the balloon rose the temperature fell by 17 degrees to ${}^-6$°C.

(c) In Sophie's experiment the temperature of the mixture was $g°$C. When she cooled it in ice the temperature fell by 21 degrees to ${}^-5$°C.

(d) One day the maximum recorded temperature in Braemar was $d°$C. The minimum was 19 degrees lower at ${}^-11$°C.

(e) The temperature in the classroom was $f°$C. When the heating system broke down the temperature fell by 21 degrees to ${}^-2$°C.

The speed limit on
motorways is 70 mph.

This car is travelling at
t mph. The driver is
speeding.

$t > 70$

This coach is travelling at
v mph. The driver is within
the speed limit.

$v \leqslant 70$

1 Write each of the following as an **inequation**.
  (a) You cook meringues at a temperature of k°C.
  The temperature must be less than 120°C.
  (b) Sarah passed her exam. She scored m marks.
  A pass was awarded for marks over 60.
  (c) Fiona is a Brownie, aged y years.
  Brownies must be 12 or under.
  (d) Hurricane Henry is blowing at d mph.
  Hurricanes blow at speeds of 75 mph or over.

2 A charter flight must obey the following rules.
  Each flight must have:
  (a) more than 220 passengers
  (b) less than 300 passengers
  (c) no more than 5 babies
  (d) at least 8 cabin staff.

  For each rule, choose a letter and write an **inequation**.

Think of a number.   ➡ n
Add 6.   ➡ $n + 6$
The result is greater than 15.   ➡ $n + 6 > 15$

The number is greater than 9. }
    The solution is } ➡ $n > 9$

---

3 For each puzzle, write an **inequation** and solve it.

(a)
Think of a number.
Add 11. The
result is more
than 15.

(b)
Think of a
number. Add 4.
The result is
less than 12.

(c)
Think of a number.
Add 8. The result
is less than 20.

(d)
Think of a
number. Subtract 5.
The result is
more than 10.

(e)
Think of a number.
Subtract 3. The
result is less
than 5.

(f)
Think of a
number. Subtract 9.
The result is
less than 8.

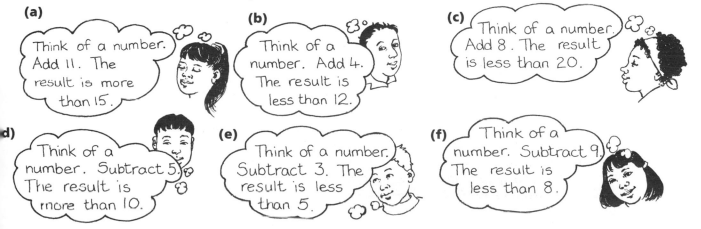

This map shows that road B1 between Ayrton and Seith is 33 miles long.

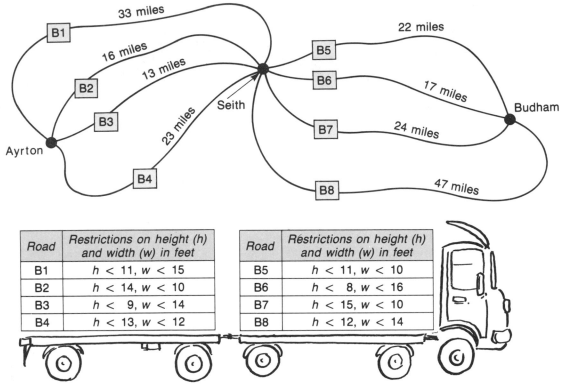

Road	Restrictions on height (h) and width (w) in feet
B1	$h < 11, w < 15$
B2	$h < 14, w < 10$
B3	$h < 9, w < 14$
B4	$h < 13, w < 12$

Road	Restrictions on height (h) and width (w) in feet
B5	$h < 11, w < 10$
B6	$h < 8, w < 16$
B7	$h < 15, w < 10$
B8	$h < 12, w < 14$

1 Find the shortest distance between Ayrton and Budham.

2 A lorry driver takes the B3 then the B5. What are the restrictions on the height and width of his load?

3 Farrenti Ltd are moving equipment from Ayrton to their new factory at Budham.
  (a) Find routes they could take for a load with a height and width of 10½ feet.
  (b) Which route would you recommend? Why?

4 Find the shortest possible route for each of these lorries.

Lorry	A	B	C	D	E	F
Height in feet	$13\frac{1}{2}$	$10\frac{1}{2}$	$8\frac{1}{2}$	$7\frac{1}{2}$	$11\frac{1}{2}$	7
Width in feet	$9\frac{1}{2}$	13	13	14	11	13

5 Farrenti Ltd advises its lorry drivers to travel at v miles per hour, where
$$v \leq 40$$
Find the shortest possible time taken by each lorry in question **4**.

Ask your teacher what to do next.

Page E1 Puzzle Corner
Issue 5 Magical Muddle

9·6	1·2	7·2
3·6	6	8·4
4·8	10·8	2·4

2·46	11·07	4·92
8·61	6·15	3·69
7·38	1·23	9·84

5·8	13·05	2·9
4·35	7·25	10·15
11·6	1·45	8·7

$2\frac{2}{5}$	$5\frac{2}{5}$	$1\frac{1}{5}$
1·8	3	4·2
$4\frac{4}{5}$	$\frac{3}{5}$	$3\frac{3}{5}$

4·4	$1\frac{9}{10}$	4·2
$3\frac{3}{10}$	$3\frac{1}{2}$	$3\frac{7}{10}$
2·8	5·1	2·6

$1\frac{4}{5}$	8·1	$3\frac{3}{5}$
$6\frac{3}{10}$	4·5	2·7
5·4	$\frac{9}{10}$	7·2

Numbers may be expressed as fractions or decimals.

Issue 11 Pathways

1 (a) 11·2 − 3·5 + 3·4   **(b)** 11·2 − 3·5 − 3·4

2 (a) 11·2 + 3·5 + 3·4 gives the largest possible target number, 18·1

  (b) 11·2 − 6·9 − 3·4 gives the smallest possible target number, 0·9

3 Answers depend on the pupil's own design for pathways puzzle.

Page E2 Apollo
1 Length of Saturn 1, 69·729 m
  Length of Saturn 5, 109·999 m
2 Length of Saturn 1 module, 4·897 m
  Length of Saturn 5 module, 4·897 m
3 1·999 m   **4** 10·059 m   **5** 2218·179 t   **6** 2·975 kg
7 £11·26 million
8 (a) £13·525 million   **(b)** £18·324 million
9 (a) £101·325 million   **(b)** £47·225 million
  (c) £9·705 million

Page E3 Moon Buggy
1 (a) Longest acceptable length, 5·247 cm
  Shortest acceptable length, 5·241 cm
  (b) 5·240 cm and 5·250 cm are not acceptable.

Issue 8 Triangular Trouble

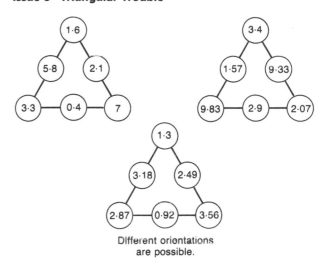

Different orientations are possible.

Page E4 disco lights
1 (a)

Pattern number	1	2	3	4	5
Number of lights	5	9	13	17	21

Formula: The number of lights is 4 times the pattern number, add 1.

2 (a) The number of lights is 4 times the pattern number.
  (b) The number of lights is 2 times the pattern number, add 6.
  (c) The number of lights is 3 times the pattern number, subtract 1.

3 Formulae depend on the pupils' own disco light patterns.

2

Moon Buggy part	Specification in cm	Shortest acceptable length in cm	Longest acceptable length in cm	Difference in cm
Bolt	5·244 ± 0·003	5·241	5·247	0·006
Washer	2·5 ± 0·004	2·496	2·504	0·008
Terminal block	15 ± 0·025	14·975	15·025	0·050
Heat sink	6·19 ± 0·035	6·155	6·225	0·070
Capacitor	3·2 ± 0·015	3·185	3·215	0·030
Blanking plate	29·5 ± 0·045	29·455	29·545	0·090

Page E5   Crossing the river

1 (a) 5 times   **(b)** 7 times   **(c)** 9 times

2

Number of people (p)	1	2	3	4	5
Number of raft crossings (c)	1	3	5	7	9

3 (a)

Number of supports (s)	2	3	4	5	6	7
Number of planks (p)	4	8	12	16	20	24

(b) Formula in words: The number of planks (p) is 4 times the number of supports (s), subtract 4.
Formula in letters: $p = 4s - 4$

Page E6   Tony the landscape gardener

1 (a)

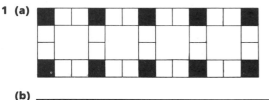

(b)

Number of flower beds (f)	1	2	3	4
Number of grey slabs (g)	4	6	8	10

Number of flower beds (f)	1	2	3	4
Number of white slabs (w)	8	14	20	26

(c) $g = 2f + 2$ $w = 6f + 2$
(d) 16 grey slabs, 74 white slabs

2 (a)

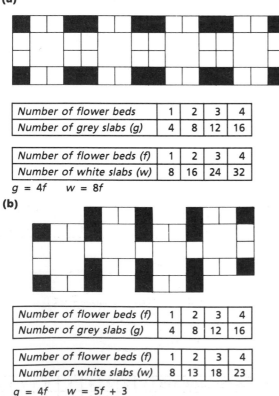

Number of flower beds	1	2	3	4
Number of grey slabs (g)	4	8	12	16

Number of flower beds (f)	1	2	3	4
Number of white slabs (w)	8	16	24	32

$g = 4f$ $w = 8f$

(b)

Number of flower beds (f)	1	2	3	4
Number of grey slabs (g)	4	8	12	16

Number of flower beds (f)	1	2	3	4
Number of white slabs (w)	8	13	18	23

$g = 4f$ $w = 5f + 3$

(c)

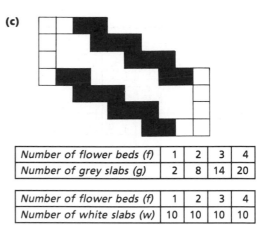

Number of flower beds (f)	1	2	3	4
Number of grey slabs (g)	2	8	14	20

Number of flower beds (f)	1	2	3	4
Number of white slabs (w)	10	10	10	10

$g = 6f - 4$ $w = 10$

3 Formula depends on pupil's own design.

Page E7   Never a cross word

1 (a)

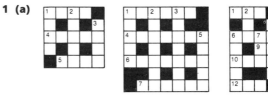

(b) 6 clues   8 clues   14 clues   16 clues
2 Answers depend on the pupil's designs.
3 The centre square.

Pages E8 and E9   Strangehill Secondary School

1 (a) Learnwell   **(b)** Roseside
2 (a) 14 more   **(b)** More came from Learnwell; 15 more
3 (a) 169 pupils   **(b)** Possible reasons might be:
• Families have recently moved into the catchment area.
• Parents outside the catchment area chose to send their children to Strangehill.
4 (a) Classes 1, 2, 3 and 4
(b) Classes 2 and 5
(c) Classes 5 and 6
5 Numbers of first year pupils not from the five schools mentioned.
6 Mrs Wong has distributed the pupils from each primary school and from elsewhere as evenly as possible over the six classes.

7

	Number of pupils						
	Class						
	1	2	3	4	5	6	Total
Croftbank	8	8	8	8	7	7	46
Gladeside	5	5	5	5	6	6	32
Learnwell	8	9	9	9	9	9	53
Parkland	4	3	4	4	3	4	22
Roseside	3	3	2	2	3	3	16
Others	2	1	1	2	1	1	8
Total	30	29	29	30	29	30	177

8 (a) Mrs Wong has allocated as far as possible an equal number of boys and girls to each class.
  (b) Answers depend on the pupil's allocations.
9 (a) 430 boys   **(b)** 365 girls   **(c)** 890 pupils
10 1986, 330 boys
11 (a) 1988   **(b)** 1980, 1981, 1982, 1986
12 (a) 1989   **(b)** 1980, 1984, 1985, 1986, 1987
13 1987. In that year there was a sharp increase in the number of pupils on the roll at Strangehill.
14 (a) Between 1983 and 1986
  (b) Between 1984 and 1986 and between 1989 and 1990.

Page E10   Photographs

1 (a), (b) The dimensions and areas of the photographs are given in this table.

w	h	A
9	1	9
8	2	16
7	3	21
6	4	24
5	5	25
4	6	24
3	7	21
2	8	16
1	9	9

  (c) The photograph with width = 5 cm and height = 5 cm has the greatest area.

2 (a)

First decimal (width)	Second decimal (height)	Total	Product (area)
0·9	0·1	1·0	0·09
0·8	0·2	1·0	0·16
0·7	0·3	1·0	0·21
0·6	0·4	1·0	0·24
0·5	0·5	1·0	0·25
0·4	0·6	1·0	0·24
0·3	0·7	1·0	0·21
0·2	0·8	1·0	0·16
0·1	0·9	1·0	0·09

3 (a) The answer depends on the pupil's predictions.
  (b) Pupils should discover that the first-place decimals which give the greatest product are 1·0 and 1·0.
4 The first-place decimals which give the greatest product are 1·5 and 1·5.
5 The greatest product occurs when the first-place decimals are the same and each is half the given total. So to find these numbers you halve the given total.

Page E11   Lengthwise

1 (a) 2 cm
  (b) 3 cm
2 (a) 3·317 cm   **(b)** 3·873 cm   **(c)** 5·292 cm
  (d) 8·426 cm
    A difference of 1 or 2 in the third decimal place is acceptable.
3 (a) 256 cm²   **(b)** 128 cm²   **(c)** 11·314 cm²
4 (a) 2 cm
  (b) 3 cm
5 (a) 2·884 cm   **(b)** 3·448 cm   **(c)** 4·291 cm
    A difference of 1 or 2 in the third decimal place is acceptable.

Page E12   The holiday camp

1

Greg	Mon	Tues	Wed	Thur	Fri
Plan 1	S	C	M	✕	✕
Plan 2	S	C	✕	✕	M
Plan 3	S	✕	M	C	✕
Plan 4	S	✕	✕	C	M
Plan 5	✕	C	S	✕	M
Plan 6	✕	✕	S	C	M

2

Fiona	Mon	Tues	Wed	Thur.	Fri
Plan 1	W	B	✕	✕	G
Plan 2	G	B	✕	W	✕
Plan 3	G	✕	✕	W	B
Plan 4	✕	B	✕	W	G

3

	Greg	Fiona
Mon	Sea fishing	Go-karting
Thur	Caves	Wildlife park
Fri	Marine park	Butterfly kingdom

These choices leave Tuesday and Wednesday free for the beach.

Page E13   Crossed lines

1 10 lines

2

Number of computers	1	2	3	4	5
Number of lines	0	1	3	6	10

3 (a) 15 lines

  (b)

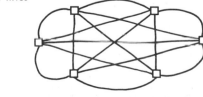

Number of computers	1	2	3	4	5	6	7	8
Number of lines	0	1	3	6	10	15	21	28

4 45 lines
5 (a) 3 lines; 6 lines
  (b) 4 lines; 10 lines
  (c) Multiply the number of computers by one less than
    the number of computers and halve the answer.
6 (a) 66 lines   **(b)** 190 lines   **(c)** 1225 lines
7 (a) Practical work.
  (b) 66 lines

Page E14   Which day?
1 Answer depends on the pupil.
2 (a) Saturday
  (b) Wednesday
  (c) Friday
  (d) Thursday
  (e) Sunday
3 (a) Saturday
  (b) Sunday
4 (a) Sunday
  (b) April and July have Black Fridays.

Page E15   Dotting about

1 (a)

Network	Number of points (p)	Number of regions (r)	$p + r$	Number of lines (l)
D	3	2	5	4
E	4	2	6	5
F	5	3	8	7
G	7	3	10	9
H	6	4	10	9

(b) $p + r$ is always 1 more than the number of lines.

(c) Number of points + number of regions =
                                  number of lines + 1
$$p + r = l + 1$$

2 (a)

Network	p	r	l
V	2	2	3
W	3	2	4
X	4	3	6
Y	5	2	6
Z	4	5	8

(b)

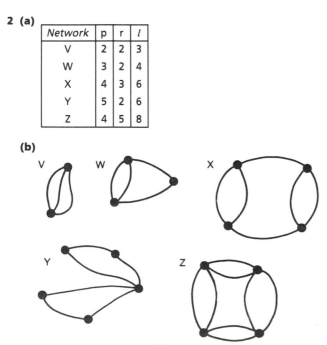

Other answers are possible.

3 (a) $p = 3$ **(b)** $r = 4$ **(c)** $l = 12$ **(d)** $r = 5$

4 (a)   **(b)**

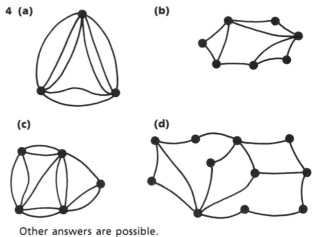

(c)   **(d)**

Other answers are possible.

Page E16   All the way round
1 (a) 110 mm   **(b)** 132 mm
2 (a) Perimeter $= 2 \times l + 2 \times b$
              $= 2l + 2b$
3 (a) 94 mm   **(b)** 134 mm   **(c)** 120 mm
4 (a) 65 cm   **(b)** 92 mm
5 (a) $P = 2 \times x + 3 \times y$
            $= 2x + 3y$
6 (a) 87 cm   **(b)** 123 mm   **(c)** 18·6 cm

Page E17   Chicken food

1

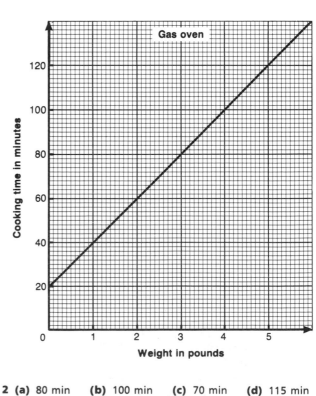

2 (a) 80 min   **(b)** 100 min   **(c)** 70 min   **(d)** 115 min
3 (a) 7.30 pm   **(b)** 6.20 pm

4

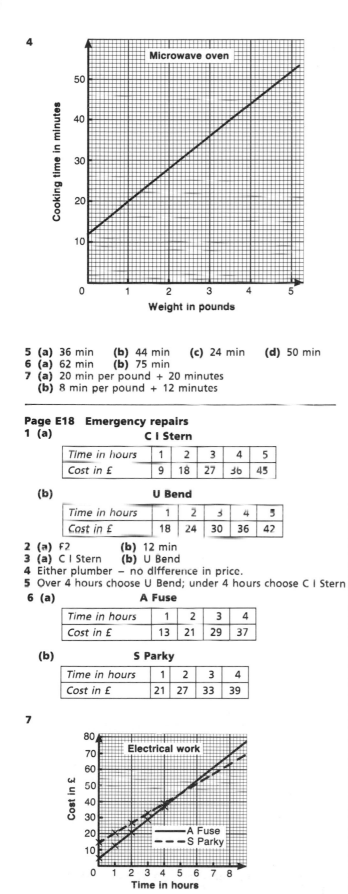

5 (a) 36 min   **(b)** 44 min   **(c)** 24 min   **(d)** 50 min
6 (a) 62 min   **(b)** 75 min
7 (a) 20 min per pound + 20 minutes
    (b) 8 min per pound + 12 minutes

Page E18   Emergency repairs
1 (a)

C I Stern

Time in hours	1	2	3	4	5
Cost in £	9	18	27	36	45

   (b)

U Bend

Time in hours	1	2	3	4	5
Cost in £	18	24	30	36	42

2 (a) £2   **(b)** 12 min
3 (a) C I Stern   **(b)** U Bend
4 Either plumber – no difference in price.
5 Over 4 hours choose U Bend; under 4 hours choose C I Stern
  6 (a)

A Fuse

Time in hours	1	2	3	4
Cost in £	13	21	29	37

   (b)

S Parky

Time in hours	1	2	3	4
Cost in £	21	27	33	39

7

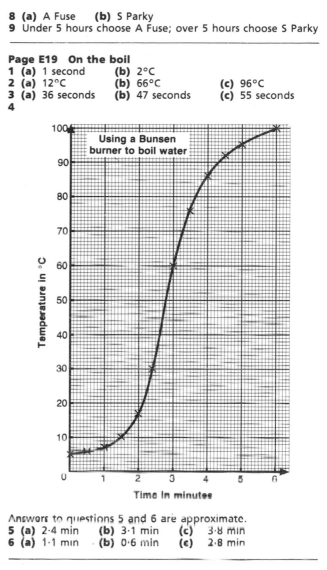

8 (a) A Fuse   **(b)** S Parky
9 Under 5 hours choose A Fuse; over 5 hours choose S Parky

Page E19   On the boil
1 (a) 1 second   **(b)** 2°C
2 (a) 12°C   **(b)** 66°C   **(c)** 96°C
3 (a) 36 seconds   **(b)** 47 seconds   **(c)** 55 seconds
4

Answers to questions 5 and 6 are approximate.
5 (a) 2·4 min   **(b)** 3·1 min   **(c)** 3·8 min
6 (a) 1·1 min   **(b)** 0·6 min   **(c)** 2·8 min

Pages E20 and E21   Movement patterns
Practical work: translation and reflection of patterns.

Page E22   Witches and wizards
1 (a) $\frac{9}{16}$ **(b)** $\frac{7}{16}$
2 (a) $\frac{1}{3}$ **(b)** $\frac{2}{3}$
3 (a) $\frac{2}{5}$ **(b)** $\frac{3}{5}$
4 (a) $\frac{1}{2}$ **(b)** $\frac{1}{4}$ **(c)** $\frac{1}{5}$ **(d)** $\frac{1}{2}$ **(e)** $\frac{3}{4}$
    (f) $\frac{2}{3}$ **(g)** $\frac{2}{3}$ **(h)** $\frac{3}{5}$ **(i)** $\frac{1}{2}$ **(j)** $\frac{3}{5}$
    (k) $\frac{1}{5}$ **(l)** $\frac{1}{4}$ **(m)** $\frac{1}{3}$ **(n)** $\frac{2}{3}$ **(o)** $\frac{1}{2}$
    (p) $\frac{2}{5}$

5 (a) $\frac{4}{15}$ **(b)** $\frac{3}{20}$ **(c)** $\frac{7}{12}$

6 (a) $\frac{11}{20}$ **(b)** $\frac{9}{100}$ **(c)** $\frac{6}{25}$

7 (a) $\frac{13}{20}$ **(b)** $\frac{7}{12}$ **(c)** $\frac{2}{3}$ **(d)** $\frac{1}{3}$

8 (a) $\frac{9}{16}$ **(b)** $\frac{7}{16}$

9 (a) $\frac{2}{5}$ **(b)** $\frac{5}{8}$ **(c)** $\frac{4}{5}$ **(d)** $\frac{4}{7}$

Page E23   Willie Wizard's Poison Potion

1 Secret juice: $2\frac{1}{5}$ cupfuls   Green gunge: $\frac{2}{5}$ cupfuls
  Sludge: $1\frac{4}{5}$ cupfuls   Super-squidge: $\frac{3}{5}$ cupfuls

2 (a) 1 cupful **(b)** $2\frac{4}{5}$ cupfuls **(c)** $5\frac{3}{5}$ cupfuls

3 (a) $\frac{1}{5}$ cupfuls **(b)** $1\frac{2}{5}$ cupfuls **(c)** $1\frac{1}{5}$ cupfuls

4 (a) $\frac{4}{5}$ **(b)** $2\frac{2}{3}$ **(c)** $3\frac{1}{2}$ **(d)** $\frac{1}{4}$ **(e)** $4\frac{1}{5}$ **(f)** $3\frac{1}{10}$

5 (a) $1\frac{1}{5}$ **(b)** $1\frac{3}{8}$ **(c)** $4\frac{1}{3}$ **(d)** $3\frac{2}{5}$ **(e)** $1\frac{1}{3}$ **(f)** $2\frac{1}{2}$
  (g) $6\frac{1}{5}$ **(h)** 5 **(i)** $4\frac{9}{16}$

6 (a) $1\frac{8}{5}$ **(b)** $2\frac{13}{8}$ **(c)** $3\frac{15}{8}$ **(d)** $1\frac{4}{3}$ **(e)** $3\frac{5}{3}$ **(f)** $1\frac{11}{6}$
  (g) $2\frac{13}{10}$ **(h)** $4\frac{7}{4}$ **(i)** $3\frac{19}{12}$ **(j)** $\frac{11}{10}$

7 (a) $2\frac{2}{3}$ **(b)** $3\frac{3}{5}$ **(c)** $1\frac{5}{8}$ **(d)** $2\frac{2}{3}$ **(e)** $1\frac{3}{5}$ **(f)** $3\frac{2}{5}$
  (g) $2\frac{2}{3}$ **(h)** $1\frac{3}{5}$ **(i)** $2\frac{3}{4}$ **(j)** $\frac{4}{5}$ **(k)** $\frac{3}{4}$ **(l)** $2\frac{1}{5}$

8 (a) $95\frac{4}{5}°C$ **(b)** $97\frac{2}{5}°C$

9 (a) $2\frac{1}{5}°C$ **(b)** $1\frac{3}{5}°C$

10 100°C

Page E24   Mandy's pie shop

1

	Strawberry	Apple	Plum	Rhubarb
Mon	$1\frac{3}{8}$	$1\frac{1}{2}$	$2\frac{3}{8}$	$\frac{7}{10}$
Tues	$1\frac{5}{8}$	$2\frac{1}{2}$	$2\frac{3}{8}$	$3\frac{3}{10}$
Wed	$3\frac{1}{8}$	$2\frac{1}{2}$	$2\frac{5}{8}$	$2\frac{2}{5}$
Thurs	$2\frac{5}{8}$	$1\frac{1}{4}$	$2\frac{5}{8}$	$2\frac{1}{10}$
Fri	$4\frac{1}{8}$	$1\frac{3}{4}$	$4\frac{1}{8}$	$3\frac{1}{2}$

2

	Strawberry	Apple	Plum	Rhubarb
(a)	$2\frac{1}{4}$	$3\frac{7}{10}$	$1\frac{5}{12}$	$1\frac{3}{4}$
(b)	$2\frac{5}{8}$	$2\frac{9}{10}$	$3\frac{1}{4}$	$2\frac{2}{3}$
(c)	$4\frac{3}{8}$	$1\frac{7}{10}$	$2\frac{1}{2}$	$3\frac{3}{4}$

3 (a) $5\frac{7}{8}$ **(b)** $1\frac{1}{2}$ **(c)** $8\frac{1}{10}$ **(d)** $3\frac{1}{2}$ **(e)** $4\frac{1}{8}$
  (f) $2\frac{1}{2}$ **(g)** $8\frac{1}{3}$ **(h)** $1\frac{3}{10}$ **(i)** $10\frac{1}{2}$ **(j)** $1\frac{1}{3}$

Page E25   Fractions graph

1 (a) 0·5 **(b)** 0·2 **(c)** 0·1 **(d)** 0·05 **(e)** 0·125
2 Answers to question 1 checked from graph.
3

	$\frac{1}{3}$	$\frac{1}{6}$	$\frac{1}{7}$	$\frac{1}{9}$	$\frac{1}{11}$	$\frac{1}{12}$	$\frac{1}{13}$	$\frac{1}{14}$	$\frac{1}{15}$	$\frac{1}{16}$	$\frac{1}{17}$	$\frac{1}{18}$	$\frac{1}{19}$
Decimal form **from the graph**	0·32	0·17	0·14	0·11	0·09	0·08	0·07	0·07	0·06	0·06	0·06	0·05	0·05
Decimal form **by calculator**	0·33	0·17	0·14	0·11	0·09	0·08	0·08	0·07	0·07	0·06	0·06	0·06	0·05

4 (a)

	$\frac{2}{3}$	$\frac{2}{5}$	$\frac{2}{7}$	$\frac{2}{9}$	$\frac{2}{11}$	$\frac{2}{13}$	$\frac{2}{15}$	$\frac{2}{17}$	$\frac{2}{19}$	$\frac{2}{21}$	$\frac{2}{23}$	$\frac{2}{25}$	$\frac{2}{27}$	$\frac{2}{29}$	$\frac{2}{31}$	$\frac{2}{33}$	$\frac{2}{35}$	$\frac{2}{37}$	$\frac{2}{39}$	$\frac{2}{40}$
Decimal form by calculator	0·67	0·40	0·29	0·22	0·18	0·15	0·13	0·12	0·11	0·10	0·09	0·08	0·07	0·07	0·06	0·06	0·06	0·05	0·05	0·05

  (b) Graph of data in **(a)**. Different scales for the axes may be used from those illustrated in question 2.
  (c) Possible answers are:
    • The graphs are the same shape.
    • For fractions with the same denominator, the decimal in the graph is double the decimal in the graph at question 2.

Page E26   New prices

1 P £36·72   Q £35·84   R £22·40   S £97·44   T £69·60
2 A £33·44   D £13·65
  B £11·05   E £5·28
  C £4·55   F £22·10

Page E27   Cable television

1 (a) 0·27, 27% **(b)** 0·68, 68% **(c)** 0·12, 12%
  (d) 0·92, 92% **(e)** 0·52, 52%
2 14%
3 15%
4 (a) 22% **(b)** 56%
5 (a) 38% **(b)** 56% **(c)** 6%
6 (a) 56% **(b)** 27% **(c)** 17%
7 (a) Practical work: Pupils' surveys.
  (b) Comparisons depend on surveys.

Page E28   The smoking percentage

1 (a) Downwards
  (b) Yes.
    Explanation could be: 'Smoking is becoming less popular'.

2

	(a)	(b)
1986	$\frac{13}{25}$	$\frac{12}{25}$
1987	$\frac{12}{25}$	$\frac{13}{25}$
1988	$\frac{49}{100}$	$\frac{51}{100}$
1989	$\frac{9}{20}$	$\frac{11}{20}$
1990	$\frac{21}{50}$	$\frac{29}{50}$

3

	(a)	(b)
1986	260	240
1987	240	260
1988	245	255
1989	225	275
1990	210	290

4

	Number of smokers in				
	1986	1987	1988	1989	1990
Male	168	146	152	129	113
Female	92	94	93	96	97
Total	260	240	245	225	210

5

	(a) male	(b) female
1986	65%	35%
1987	61%	39%
1988	62%	38%
1989	57%	43%
1990	54%	46%

6

	(a) male	(b) female
1986	67%	37%
1987	58%	38%
1988	61%	37%
1989	52%	38%
1990	45%	39%

7 (a) Pupils should produce different types of graphs; for example, compound bar graphs or trend graphs.
(b) Pupils write about their graphs.
8 Practical work: pupils' surveys.

Page E29   Eric's designs

1 (a)
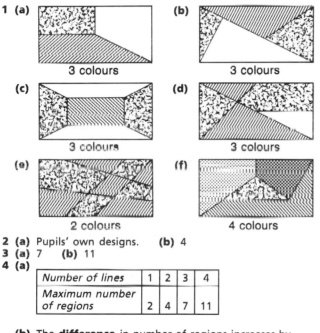
3 colours

(b) 3 colours

(c) 3 colours

(d) 3 colours

(e) 2 colours

(f) 4 colours

2 (a) Pupils' own designs.   **(b)** 4
3 (a) 7   **(b)** 11
4 (a)

Number of lines	1	2	3	4
Maximum number of regions	2	4	7	11

(b) The **difference** in number of regions increases by one for each new line.
(c) 16
(d) Diagram confirming 16 regions.
(e) Each line must cross every other line avoiding existing intersections.
5 Only **2** colours are needed.

Page E30   Polygons

1 (a) P 5 sides, 5 angles   **Q** 4 sides, 4 angles
R 6 sides, 6 angles,   **S** 3 sides, 3 angles
T 8 sides, 8 angles
(b) 12
2 (a) Pupils' own answers.
(b) P, **Q**, **S** and **T**.
(c) • Equilateral triangle • square • regular pentagon
3 (a) 60°   **(b)** 45°   **(c)** 40°   **(d)** 36°

Page E31   Regular polygons

Practical work: constructing regular polygons.

Page E32   Mystic cubes

1

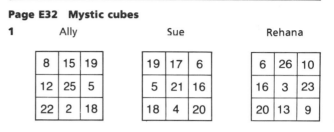

Ally

8	15	19
12	25	5
22	2	18

Sue

19	17	6
5	21	16
18	4	20

Rehana

6	26	10
16	3	23
20	13	9

2 (a) The numbers on each row and column sum to the same total.
(b) The sum of the numbers on the diagonals is different from those on the rows and columns.

3

Top

26	15	1
6	19	17
10	8	24

Bottom

18	20	4
22	9	11
2	13	27

10	8	24
5	21	16
27	13	2

26	6	10
12	25	5
4	11	27

1	15	26
23	7	12
18	20	4

24	17	1
16	3	23
2	22	18

4 (a)

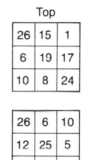

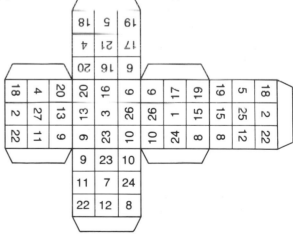

(b) Answers depend on the orientation of the cube when choosing layers.

Page E33   Oil rigs

1 Burpo 1: 500 km   Burpo 2: 400 km   Burpo 3: 325 km
2

Time	½ hour	1 hour	2 hours	5 hours	7 hours
Distance	10 km	20 km	40 km	100 km	140 km

3 (a) 25 hours   **(b)** 20 hours
4 (a) 200 km   **(b)** 10 hours
5

Time	1 hour	2 hours	3 hours	4 hours	6 hours
Distance	150 km	300 km	450 km	600 km	900 km

6 (a) 30 minutes   **(b)** 20 minutes   **(c)** 10 minutes
7 (a) 3 hr 20 min   **(b)** 2 hr 40 min
    (c) 2 hr 10 min   **(d)** 7 hr 20 min
8 (a) 2315   **(b)** 0200 on Friday

Page E34   Move it to the right . . .

1

Vertex	P	Q	R
○ Circle	(2,5)	(6,5)	(12,5)
× Cross	(1,3)	(5,3)	(11,3)
■ Square	(4,2)	(8,2)	(14,2)

2 (2,5) moves to (6,5) so 2+4=6
   (1,3) moves to (5,3) so 1+4=5
   (4,2) moves to (8,2) so 4+4=8
3 (a) (6,5) moves to (12,5) so 6+6=12
    (8,2) moves to (14,2) so 8+6=14
    (5,3) moves to (11,3) so 5+6=11
  (b) (2,5) moves to (12,5) so 2+10=12
    (4,2) moves to (14,2) so 4+10=14
    (1,3) moves to (11,3) so 1+10=11
4

Vertex	P	Q	R
○ Circle	(⁻6, 4)	(⁻1, 4)	(6, 4)
■ Square	(⁻4, 3)	(1, 3)	(8, 3)
× Cross	(⁻3, 1)	(2, 1)	(9, 1)
▲ Triangle	(⁻8,⁻1)	(⁻3,⁻1)	(4,⁻1)

5 (⁻6, 4) ⟶ (⁻1,4) so ⁻6+5=⁻1
   (⁻4, 3) ⟶ (1,3) so ⁻4+5= 1
   (⁻3, 1) ⟶ (2,1) so ⁻3+5= 2
   (⁻8,⁻1) ⟶ (⁻3,1) so ⁻8+5=⁻3
6 (a) (⁻1, 4) ⟶ (6, 4) so ⁻1+7=6
    (1, 3) ⟶ (8, 3) so 1+7=8
    (2, 1) ⟶ (9, 1) so 2+7=9
    (⁻3,⁻1) ⟶ (4,⁻1) so ⁻3+7=4
  (b) (⁻6, 4) ⟶ (6, 4) so ⁻6+12=6
    (⁻4, 3) ⟶ (8, 3) so ⁻4+12=8
    (⁻3, 1) ⟶ (9, 1) so ⁻3+12=9
    (⁻8,⁻1) ⟶ (4,⁻1) so ⁻8+12=4
7 (a) K(3,1)   L(⁻1,3)   M(⁻3,⁻1)   N(1,⁻3)
  (b) K(9,1)   L(5,3)   M(3,⁻1)   N(7,⁻3)
8 (a) ⁻6+4=⁻2   **(b)** 0+5= 5   **(c)** ⁻1+3=2
  (d) 2+6= 8   **(e)** ⁻9+7=⁻2   **(f)** ⁻3+6=3
  (g) ⁻2+1=⁻1   **(h)** ⁻10+8=⁻2   **(i)** ⁻5+5=0

Page E35   Move it to the left . . .

1

Vertex	P	Q	R
○ Circle	(8,5)	(1,5)	(⁻5,5)
■ Square	(9,1)	(2,1)	(⁻4,1)
× Cross	(6,2)	(⁻1,2)	(⁻7,2)

2 (8,5) moves to (1,5) so 8−7= 1
   (9,1) moves to (2,1) so 9−7= 2
   (6,2) moves to (⁻1,2) so 6−7=⁻1

3 (a) (1, 5) moves to (⁻5,5) so   1−6=⁻5
    (2, 1) moves to (⁻4, 1) so   2−6=⁻4
    (⁻1, 2) moves to (⁻7,2) so ⁻1−6=⁻7
  (b) (8,5) moves to (⁻5,5) so 8−13=⁻5
    (9,1) moves to (⁻4,1) so 9−13=⁻4
    (6,2) moves to (⁻7,2) so 6−13=⁻7

4

Vertex	P	Q	R
○ Circle	(10, 2)	(2, 2)	(⁻3, 2)
■ Square	(8,⁻3)	(0,⁻3)	(⁻5,⁻3)
× Cross	(5,⁻2)	(⁻3,⁻2)	(⁻8,⁻2)
▲ Triangle	(7, 3)	(⁻1, 3)	(⁻6, 3)

5 (10, 2) moves to (2, 2) so 10−8= 2
   (8,⁻3) moves to (0,⁻3) so   8−8= 0
   (5,⁻2) moves to (⁻3,⁻2) so   5−8=⁻3
   (7, 3) moves to (⁻1, 3) so   7−8=⁻1
6 (a) (2, 2) moves to (⁻3,⁻2) so   2−5= 3
    (0,⁻3) moves to (⁻5,⁻3) so   0−5=⁻5
    (⁻3,⁻2) moves to (⁻8,⁻2) so ⁻3−5=⁻8
    (⁻1, 3) moves to (⁻6, 3) so ⁻1−5=⁻6
  (b) (10, 2) moves to (⁻3, 2) so 10−13=⁻3
    (8,⁻3) moves to (⁻5,⁻3) so 8−13=⁻5
    (5,⁻2) moves to (⁻8,⁻2) so 5−13=⁻8
    (7, 3) moves to (⁻6, 3) so 7−13=⁻6
7 (a) K(0,3)   L(⁻4,3)   M(⁻6,⁻1)   N(⁻2,⁻1)
  (b) K(⁻4,3)   L(⁻8,3)   M(⁻10,⁻1)   N(⁻6,⁻1)
8 (a) ⁻6−1= ⁻7   **(b)** 8− 7= 1   **(c)** 5−9= ⁻4
  (d) ⁻2−4= ⁻6   **(e)** 3− 5=⁻2   **(f)** 0−6=⁻6
  (g) ⁻7−3=⁻10   **(h)** 4−12=⁻8   **(i)** ⁻2−9=⁻11

Page E36   Hot and cold

1 (a) x + 5 =   3   **(b)** g + 17 = 12   **(c)** n + 31 = 24
      x = ⁻2   g = ⁻5   n = ⁻7
  (d) w + 29 = 23   **(e)** t + 25 = ⁻2
      w = ⁻6   t = ⁻27
2 (a) f − 25 = ⁻8   **(b)** b − 17 = ⁻6   **(c)** g − 21 = ⁻5
      f = 17   b = 11   g = 16
  (d) d − 19 = ⁻11   **(e)** f − 21 = ⁻2
      d = 8   f = 19

Page E37   Keeping to the limits

1 (a) t < 120   **(b)** m > 60   **(c)** y ⩽ 12   **(d)** d ⩾ 75
2 Pupils choose their own letter for each.
  (a) p > 220   **(b)** p < 300   **(c)** b ⩽ 5   **(d)** s ⩾ 8
3 (a) n + 11 > 15   **(b)** n + 4 < 12   **(c)** n + 8 < 20
      n > 4   n < 8   n < 12
  (d) n − 5 > 10   **(e)** n − 3 < 5   **(f)** n − 9 < 8
      n > 15   n < 8   n < 17

Page E38   Routes

1 B3 then B6, 30 miles
2 h < 9, w < 10
3 (a) B1 or B4 then B8
  (b) Pupil's own reasons which might include:
    • B4 then B8 is shorter
    • B1 then B8 gives the wider choice of route.
4 A B2 then B7, 40 miles
   B B1 then B8, 80 miles
   C B3 then B8, 60 miles
   D B1 then B6, 50 miles
   E B4 then B8, 70 miles
   F B3 then B6, 30 miles
5 A 1 hour   B 2 hours   C 1½ hours   D 1¼ hours
   E 1 hour 45 minutes   F 45 minutes